RENEWAL IN THE
WILDERNESS

A Spiritual Guide to Connecting with God in the Natural World

John Lionberger

Walking Together, Finding the Way ®
SKYLIGHT PATHS®
PUBLISHING
Woodstock, Vermont

Renewal in the Wilderness:
A Spiritual Guide to Connecting with God in the Natural World

2007 First Printing
© 2007 by John Lionberger

Library of Congress Cataloging-in-Publication Data
Lionberger, John.
Renewal in the wilderness : a spiritual guide to connecting with God in the natural world / John Lionberger.
    p. cm.
Includes bibliographical references.
ISBN-13: 978-1-59473-219-5 (pbk.)
ISBN-10: 1-59473-219-1 (pbk.)
1. Nature—Religious aspects. 2. Spiritual life. I. Title.

BL65.N35L56   2007
204—dc22
                                                                    2007010444

10 9 8 7 6 5 4 3 2 1

Manufactured in the United States of America

Cover Design: Melanie Robinson

SkyLight Paths Publishing is creating a place where people of different spiritual traditions come together for challenge and inspiration, a place where we can help each other understand the mystery that lies at the heart of our existence. SkyLight Paths sees both believers and seekers as a community that increasingly transcends traditional boundaries of religion and denomination—people wanting to learn from each other, *walking together, finding the way.*®

SkyLight Paths, "Walking Together, Finding the Way" and colophon are trademarks of LongHill Partners, Inc., registered in the U.S. Patent and Trademark Office.

Walking Together, Finding the Way®
Published by SkyLight Paths Publishing
A Division of LongHill Partners, Inc.
Sunset Farm Offices, Route 4, P.O. Box 237
Woodstock, VT 05091
Tel: (802) 457-4000   Fax: (802) 457-4004
www.skylightpaths.com

To my wife, Jane,
who has been more responsible than any
human for my spiritual life,
and who reflects God's grace so eloquently;
and to God, who surprised (and continues
to surprise) the living daylights out of me ...
often in the wilderness, often not.

CONTENTS

CONTENTS

ACKNOWLEDGMENTS

Despite the image of a writer toiling alone in a garret, books are simply not the work of just one person. There's a small troop of people offering support and encouragement when the slogging gets tough, and prodding when it's needed. For example, volunteers who read the budding chapters and point out where things don't make sense or get preachy. Editors, who take the rough manuscript and turn it into a silk purse: whatever they are paid is certainly not enough. Wondrous spouses, who tolerate the suffering artist. And friends, who are truly interested in the author's progress.

So, profuse thanks to the following:

Wondrous Spouse: My amazing Jane.

Readers: Pamela Toler, Kay Art, Kay Sturm, and Catherine Wallace.

Editors: Marcia Broucek and Emily Wichland. If I were wearing a hat, I'd take it off to you both.

Friends: You know who you are.

Contributors: Your insights and comments helped shape the book.

And special thanks to Laura Fredrickson Moeller and Dorothy Anderson, who allowed me unlimited use of their seminal study of the wilderness experience as a source of spiritual inspiration.

INTRODUCTION

Life is either a daring adventure or nothing at all.
                              —*Helen Keller (1880–1968)*

Given the level of creature comforts we've achieved in North America, it may seem like a fool's errand to head out into the wilderness. We've worked very hard to be comfortable, so why would we trade our flip-of-the-switch temperature control for whatever temperature nature throws at us? A solid house for a thin tent? A comfortable bed for a sleeping bag and an air mattress? Our daily showers and flush toilets for, well, *not* daily showers and flush toilets? Why should we, as creatures accustomed to our ease, think about going into the wilderness where things are not easy?

> *What have I just committed to? A canoe trip? At my age? Endurance? Forget it. The last time I paddled was thirty years ago, in college, when I was young, virile, and fearless. And canoeing in October in the middle of Wisconsin? That's when the leaves fall, when the air is cold, when the water is cold. What if it rains? How will I ever stay warm if I get wet?*

Most people wrestle with these kinds of doubts when they contemplate taking a wilderness trip. But when Rob Davis pursued his long-delayed dream of another wilderness adventure—this time

1

taking a three-day trip on the Wisconsin River—his actual experience sums up why it's worth it to leave our comforts for a short while, to be in the wilderness, to be away from the busyness of normal living, to return to the slower rhythm and tranquility of nature:

> *Suddenly, here we are on the river. I'm not an experienced paddler, but as I get the hang of it, I begin to look around. Spread out before me is a beautiful, peaceful river. And I'm not only staying warm, but I'm having fun.*
>
> *After we find a place to camp and have a wonderful meal, the dark settles in and the night begins to get cold. As we huddle around the campfire, an amazing thing happens: We begin to talk. We are strangers to each other, but we begin to open up. Maybe we talk because it's cold and we're feeling vulnerable. Maybe it's because we're far from civilization where we've built walls to make us feel secure.*
>
> *On this island in the middle of nowhere, we create an island of light in the darkness. We talk about life's pains and struggles. We talk about our spirituality. No two of us have the same view. The discussion is deliberate, emotional, and meaningful; not the quick-paced, short snippets of conversation you might have over a beer. We talk for hours, stoking the fire, and adding another layer of clothing every so often. The night is glorious. The stars are shining bright and remind me of nights at my family's cabin. But none seem better than this.*
>
> *On the ride back home, I'm exhausted, but my head is filled with wonderful memories. I pushed my body harder than I have in years, and I felt closer to God and the people with whom I've shared this wilderness experience.*

One of the laws of nature says that for every action there's an opposite and equal reaction, and that applies to our disconnect from the wilderness as well: In gaining our comforts, we have lost much of our ancient and intimate connection with nature, with ourselves, and finally, with God. John Calvin once said that nature is "the theater of God's glory." If you believe, as I do, that nature is God's oldest, perhaps purest, work on this earth, then in our isolation from nature we have lost that direct, personal connection to the theater of the holy. We see nature through the window but have little direct involvement because we are not "in" it. Our concept of the Divine becomes centered almost completely in our head, in our intellect.

But it belongs, instead, in our heart. This is important because we respond to the wilderness far more with the heart than with the head. In the wilderness, our hearts are opened; it is there that our hearts, rather than our minds, acquire the eyes that see.

I have a very personal interest in this because of my ministry, Renewal in the Wilderness. I take people—mostly middle-aged people (like Rob) who lost their Olympic conditioning years ago—into the wilderness for trips of spiritual renewal and exploration. I do this because a wilderness experience of my own compelled me to abandon a lifetime of angry agnosticism to go into the ministry after many years in business. I know intimately how the wilderness can change a person. Thoreau once said that the salvation of the world is in the wilderness, and in human aspects, I believe to my marrow that he was right.

Over and over again, I've witnessed the power of the wilderness to affect the lives of people willing to relinquish some creature comforts and (frequently) their Type A behavior, and go to a wild place in the hope of encountering God. Whether Jewish or Christian or Buddhist or agnostic or whatever, people have remarkably similar experiences: They become more as a child, seeing everything as charged with wonder and excitement. Whatever their religious persuasion, they find Something Bigger Than I Am. For some, the wilderness trips become catalysts for life renewal.

What makes the wilderness so uniquely effective in bringing people into a more intimate relationship with God? Why, for thousands of years, have people who longed for intimate spiritual connection left the comforts (and false surety) of civilization to go into the wilderness?

First, the wilderness stretches our physical and spiritual boundaries, opening us up to the possibility of radical changes.

Second, the impulse to see and be in a natural setting when we want to be in communion with God seems to be universal, as if it's in our DNA. Religions across the world and across great spans of time have recognized the power of the wilderness to bring people into authentic and personal relationships with the Divine. Many of the stories and quotations throughout this book show how ancient and widespread this wilderness/spiritual impulse is.

Third, the very unfamiliarity of the wilderness environment keeps us in the present moment, keenly aware of nearly everything. There is nothing we can take for granted, so we have to think intentionally about everything we do. And it is at these times, when we're so totally present, that God can get through to us.

Fourth, the wilderness is God's "hull-scraper"; it strips us of the barnacles of civilization that slow us, distract us, and divert us in our pursuit of God—and God's pursuit of us.

Fifth, in freeing us of our civilized "barriers," the wilderness breaks down the walls of expectation we've created to contain God—and ourselves. The door opens for God to woo us and wow us—and for us to recognize that we are being courted.

Sixth, when things aren't quite so comfortable or predictable, when we are in unfamiliar territory that is so vast and we feel so small, we come to realize both our finitude and God's infinitude. God is most often found at the edges, in the places where our civilized niceties lose their grip and we realize, finally, that we are not in control.

Seventh, an important part of nearly every religious tradition is intentional periods of solitude and silence. The wilderness encourages and rewards both, and both allow us to spend intimate time with ourselves and with God.

Eighth, God's wild places allow us to live with more open, honest hearts than civilized places ever seem to allow. Actually, I think wild places *demand* that we live with open and honest hearts. In the wilderness we can move beyond what the rational mind can explain to experience the transcendent, to rediscover a life-renewing joy in being alive.

The bottom line is this: If we want to be with the God who created us, rather than the God we create, we need to be in a place that reminds us of who God is, of who we are (and also of who we are not), and how much we need each other. For many, that place of encounter and transformation is the wilderness.

I am passionate about the spiritual possibilities in the wilderness, and so are others (as you'll see in the stories that follow) who took the opportunity to leave their comforts behind for a short time to have their lives touched and changed by their meetings with God in the wilderness. I encourage you to make use of the Questions for Reflection at the end of each chapter to consider what renewal in the wilderness might hold for you. You may find it helpful to journal about these questions (you can use the spaces within this book if you'd like), and if you decide to do this, I encourage you to turn off your internal "editor" so that the words just flow and accurately reflect your reactions and the feelings that arise. The questions are also excellent for group discussions.

While this book is almost exclusively about the natural wilderness, it is important to recognize that there are other wildernesses—such as addiction, prison, sickness, the process of dying, aging, divorce, job loss, and spiritual dryness—that put us on the edges of our lives. As both a hospital chaplain and a retirement home chaplain, I've had, and been with others who have had, experiences of God's presence and involvement that equal those of true wilderness journeys, challenges that have strengthened our respective belief in God's existence and involvement in our lives.

I believe that wilderness is a place of infinite invitation and renewal. *Any* wilderness can create the spaces for us to have a very different awareness of, and relationship with, God. While my passion is for the truly remote and wild places, I know that some people simply cannot get there. For those folks, please know that much of what this book talks about can be found in city parks or in walks around the block—if you go to those places with awareness, open to surprise. There is a large and beautiful park not far from my home, and many times in the process of writing this book, I've retreated there to get away from the "wilderness" of writing, away from the traffic in my own head, to watch the geese and ducks in the pond. Their only agenda is "right now," and I envy them. They teach me "right now" again, because I forget. I can also smell the flowers and feel the breezes, and in that reminder of a different rhythm and priority, I decompress. When I leave the park, I am refreshed and reconnected. God's presence is very much *present.*

Regardless of what's available to you, I hope you'll be encouraged to stop saying that you can't take the time to "get out there" ... because there are things at home that need doing, there's not enough time or money, you're too out of shape, or whatever the excuses might be—and they are usually excuses, not good reasons. It is a given that none of us is getting younger, and at a certain point it will, in fact, become too late to go on a spiritual adventure of this kind, and our excuses for not going to the wilderness *will* become real reasons. Life *is* short, and *tempus* is *fugiting.* If we let our self-imposed limits become permanent, inertia has won.

So, to those who would consider giving up their civilized comforts for a few days for the possibility that their lives might change forever, I offer this book.

NOTES

GOD IN A HUMMINGBIRD
THE WILDERNESS IS A PLACE OF TRANSFORMATION.

RENEWAL IN THE WILDERNESS

The closer we are to Nature, the closer we are to God.
—*Johann Wolfgang von Goethe (1749–1842),*
German poet, writer, painter, philosopher

Springtime along the Rio Grande in the Big Bend National Park of Texas is stunning in a way I never expected. For a boy from the Midwest, where the word *beautiful* implicitly means everything's green, the deep desert is a jarring contrast. There's not much that's verdant. Rather, it's all shades of gray, brown, ocher, and black. Once we adapt to the idea that little here is green, we realize, almost to our surprise, that this is truly beautiful country. Hauntingly so, for it is so hard, so silent, and so astonishingly basic.

I'm leading a group on a Renewal in the Wilderness trip, and we're canoeing through ancient three-hundred-foot-high canyons. They're deep oxblood in color at best, charred black at worst, as if the sun has either scalded or blowtorched them. They even look hot to the touch, which, thinking ahead to summer, doesn't seem like such a reach. It's only late February, but even now the sun is intense. We can't imagine what July must be like, but the term *blast furnace* is not far from our thoughts.

This, however, is the rainy season, and there's been enough moisture that waxy-looking, thick-petaled yellow and white flowers are blooming on the crowns of all the varieties of cacti. The petals appear succulent, chewy, and cool, and in some magical places at breaks in the canyon walls, we see delicate carpets of very light-purple ground flowers that look gauzy from a distance, like a mirage. They're hazy, shimmering, and amorphous, as if they perhaps don't exist; they're the desert-flower version of Brigadoon, and we have to look several times to be sure they're really there. These flowers are so unexpected, such a treat to behold, that we tread very carefully when we beach the canoes for rest breaks or to camp, so that we spare them our crushing feet; they already have enough to deal with in this desert. The delicacy amid the brutal, the toughness of life, and the astonishing diversity and ingenuity of creation isn't lost on any of us.

We're here to find God.

This either sounds grandiose or presumptuous, depending on how you interpret it. Whichever the interpretation, I shake my head in wonder, and sometimes disbelief, because those words, coming from me, are a measure of how radically my life has changed because of my own experiences in the wilderness. In 1995, as a dedicated agnostic, I went into the wilderness for an adventure but came out knowing I'd been profoundly touched by God. Religious people would say I was transformed. I'd say I was ambushed, in the best possible meaning of that word.

AMBUSHED BY GOD

> Try and penetrate ... the secrets of nature ... and you will
> find something ... inexplicable. Veneration for this force
> beyond anything that we can comprehend is my religion.
> —*Albert Einstein (1879–1955)*

The north woods of Minnesota are achingly beautiful at any time
of year. I've been here on canoe trips in the summer, and each time
I've been awed by the haunting call of loons; the pure pine-
fragrant air; the flinty hardness of the ancient rocks; the cold,
clean, dark water; the night sky so lush with stars you think you
are in a better universe; the profound quiet. It's a place that seeps
into your heart and wraps around your memory. It renews your
soul—even if you don't believe in God—and it refreshes your perspective on life.

But as beautiful as the north woods are in warmer months,
they pale in comparison to their blinding beauty on a sunny winter day.

I'm here because my wife loves me. And knows me. I've just
celebrated a milestone birthday, and as a gift Jane has given me the
hardest seven-day trip that Outward Bound offers: a heart-of-the-
winter, weeklong dogsledding expedition in the Boundary Waters
Canoe Area of northern Minnesota.

I love challenges like this because they expand my understanding of who I am and what I'm capable of, but at the moment
I'm wondering whether I'm capable of withstanding the minus-
forty-degree temperatures that northern Minnesota often sees. I'd
be a fool not to be concerned. As I look around at my fellow travelers, I know that I'm not the only one.

Anxiety is very apparent in the eyes and body language of
most of the group. There's a lot of nervous laughter and awkward
joking as we sit on our bunks or stand around the potbellied stove
that heats our very spare cabin, waiting for our instructors. Most

of the jokes are about the cold; some are gallows humor about giving permission to the survivors to eat the corpses of those who perish. "I've never done anything like this," one says. Another comments, "My friends and my children all think I'm out of my mind," and there's a lot of agreement. A slender man from New York City says slowly, with gravity and the deepest "gladiator" voice he can summon, "We who are about to die salute you." Anything to alleviate the tension. Those of us who pray—and I am not one of them—silently plead that the instructors know their business because we know that these conditions can quickly be lethal if serious mistakes are made.

We're all strangers in this group, and all middle-aged, for this is a "thirty-five or older" trip that Outward Bound put together for adults who don't want to be surrounded by—or intimidated by—the hormones and/or endurance of the teenagers that Outward Bound more famously takes into the wilderness. We're equally split by gender, and we've come from all over the country for this adventure. We want to see what we're made of, to get outside whatever boxes we've allowed to define our lives.

The Outward Bound literature had described the course as "travel by ski and dogsled across snow-covered lakes." Though we know it is not going to be an Iditarod experience, most of us are still harboring the powerfully romantic image of standing on the runners of a taut racing sled, shouting instructions to the willing dogs as they rip us over the snow at twenty miles an hour. It was not to be.

There *are* dogs, but only five of them, and they are pulling a huge cargo sled that carries about three hundred pounds of food for humans and dogs; a ten-by-twelve-foot sidewall cooking tent for meals; cooking gear (including a heat-shielding platform for the stove so it won't go through the ice); a five-foot-long, twenty-pound iron rod to break through the two-foot-thick ice so we can get water; shovels; repair equipment; a satellite telephone; and the backpacks of those mushing the dogs for the day. Fully loaded, the sled weighs about six hundred pounds.

The rest of us are on wide back-country skis, carrying full-sized expedition packs filled with our clothing, personal effects, and sleeping gear. Our job is to help the dogs by breaking trail through the snow, either overland among all the pines and low scrub trees, or across the many frozen lakes. We quickly become adept at spotting the wet places on the lakes where water has seeped into the snow. Not only does the slush cake the sled runners and our skis with slush ice that has to be scraped off, but also, more critically, someone could easily fall through. We've practiced ice rescue, and we know what to do if it happens, but no one wants to be that person. We've been taught how to test ice for structural integrity, and we're damned serious about it.

Now that we're under way, the nervousness has ended. In the act of *doing* the adventure, we're *in* the adventure, and most of us find that our expectations of severe hardship far exceed the reality.

It's simply gorgeous out here. The cold in northern Minnesota is ... astonishing; there's simply no other word for it. It grabs your attention immediately. The hip-high blanket of snow reflects the sunlight from the trillions of crystals that cover the ground, as if all the stars of the universe have fallen to earth and are twinkling. The boughs of the pine trees extend their captured plumps of snow the way a good waiter presents a fine wine: with dignity, flair, and a sense of abundance. And when the wind blows, the tree-held snow falls again in miniature blizzards of sparkle. The sky is more intensely cobalt blue than you would think possible, as if the color had been invented, then perfected, here. It's a majestic place, and it feels like wintry creation.

At our first campsite, after we unload the sled and begin to set up our cook tent, someone asks, "Where are *our* tents?" There is mild concern in her voice, and her tone and the question itself catches everyone's attention. The instructors—Don and Sue—have been waiting patiently for this moment. They're bent over a task, so no one notices their Mona Lisa smiles.

"I'm sorry," Don says innocently, "what was the question?"

"Where are *our* tents?" There was a dramatic silence.

"Your tents?! Oh, yes ... well! Well, you see ... we'll be sleeping outside," Don says offhandedly as he and Sue continue to work, bent over, eyes focused on their project. Wider smiles.

We all stop what we're doing and stand straight up; even the wind ceases. It's silent as a pillow.

"What?" Long pause.

"Oh ... did we forget to tell you?" Sue asks casually, as if it's an insignificant oversight. They continue to work while we stand in disbelief. "We sleep outside in the winter, you know. Don't have to worry about mosquitoes, do we!" Brief, stunned silence as we take this in.

"What??!!!" More voices in the chorus.

"Oh sure, you betcha," Sue says in her best Minnesota accent, standing up, finally, with a huge ear-to-ear grin. "We sleep under tarps in case it snows, eh, but outside, don'tcha know."

Seeing our stunned disbelief, Don adds, laughing, "Tents build up too much ice with body condensation, so we just leave 'em for the summer. We double bag ya, though, so ya sleep warm."

"Double bag" means stuffing one sleeping bag inside the other, and the instructors are right: The arrangement works beautifully. The first night is interesting, though, as we come to grips with the magnificent cold, and who will sleep at the two ends of the sardine body-to-body sleeping configuration. Those two people won't have the benefit of someone else's body heat on one side, and it's a serious matter. We have a major discussion about who has the highest metabolism, and the man from New York, who's a marathoner, and I get the ends. Most of us sleep very soundly, despite the profound cold, except those who hadn't eaten enough of the high-fat dinner that helps us sleep warm. It's a mistake they don't repeat for the rest of the trip.

Travel the next day is basically a repeat of the first day, but more efficient because we've already learned a lot about packing, dog-handling, mushing, skiing, pack-carrying, and path-picking across the lakes to avoid the wet spots. The sky is heavily overcast, and the woods and lakes look very different because of the flatter light. The wilderness is not so starkly etched by strong shadows and deep color contrasts between the egret-white snow, deep-green pines, and gray-black rock outcroppings. Everything looks much softer, though no less beautiful.

This is a longer, harder day than the one before. One person in our group is having trouble, and though we divvy up much of the weight in her pack to make it easier, she's still struggling. About thirty minutes from our next campsite, she has to drop her pack in the middle of Knife Lake; she skis on without it.

After we arrive at our new campsite and get the sleeping tarps and cook tent set up, I volunteer to go back and get her pack. I enjoy people's company, but I'm an introvert by nature, so I relish time alone. Especially when I can be alone in a place like this. The sun is arcing slowly downward—it will be gone in about an hour—and the temperature is dropping as well; not quickly yet, but it will begin to nose-dive once the sun nears about fifteen degrees off the horizon. Making sure I have my headlamp and a whistle, just in case, the instructors let me go, cautioning me not to leave the trail. It should take me about forty-five minutes, round-trip, if I hustle.

It's good to be alone; the solitude is refreshing and welcome. My pace is just below the sweat threshold, but faster than we'd skied all day since I'm carrying nothing but water, and I'm skiing in the tracks we've already made. The light is becoming dis-cernibly flatter, the landscape colors beginning to bleed into stronger monotone hues. There's an imperative to make prudent haste, so I don't dawdle. The wind has quieted, so the only sound I hear is my own breathing, the "poosh" sound of my ski poles punching holes in the snow, and the hiss of my skis. This is truly sublime, and I am feeling very content, very peaceful.

About twenty minutes later, I find the abandoned pack, but the setting is too serene to head back just yet; the moment is too rare. So I stand there appreciating the silence, the solitude, and the beauty, wanting to absorb it into my marrow. I linger because there's a poignancy in being here, a bracing melancholy, a quiet beauty I hunger for. I want to soak up its enormity because there is nothing like it back in the city.

Looking around, I realize the only sign of humanity I can see is my own tracks in the snow, and I'm quickly reminded that I am very alone. It makes me feel small in proportion to the vastness of the place. My fingers are beginning to tingle, and I know I should be moving to generate some body heat, but I stand rooted to that spot, transfixed.

I look at the small thermometer on the zipper of my anorak; the temperature has fallen about twenty-five degrees in the past hour and now stands at fifteen below. I'm still relatively comfortable, but I can feel the fangs of the cold beginning to come through my clothing. Though I'm physically aware of the cold, I'm feeling warmly content and connected to everything, including myself. Deep breath ... cold air in my lungs ... the trees, the rock outcroppings, the shoreline beginning to turn purplish as the light dims further. The hard edges will soon be black in the late twilight, the pines and aspen silhouetted strongly against the sky.

It will be dark before I get back to camp, and I don't want to cause concern among the others, but I'm still reluctant to leave, so I allow myself five more minutes to silently steep in the experience. I close my eyes and point my face at the sky; I lift my arms to shoulder height, parallel to the ground, with the ski poles dangling from my wrists, back arched, standing in the middle of that frozen lake as the temperature and daylight continue to drop.

In that posture, and in that cold, without warning, I am suddenly overwhelmed with the sense that I'm standing in a shower stream of pure and profound warmth, from the inside out. A sense of peace that's bone-true and javelin-straight floods me, dwarfing any similar sensation I've ever had. My eyes shoot open to see what's causing this sensation of pure warmth, but there is nothing to see except the darkening sky.

I don't have even the *hint* of a clue about what's happening, but whatever "it" is, it is perfect, and goes straight to my heart. I feel utterly cared for.

As the feeling slowly recedes, my arms reluctantly drop back to my sides, and my head comes slowly back to level. I look down to see whether there might be a puddle of melt-water at my feet, but there isn't one. I shake my head to clear it and look around. Nothing has changed, but something has just happened that I cannot explain.

As a grandson of Missouri—the "show me" state—I want an explanation, but there is none. "Am I going hypothermic?" I wonder. "Was that a small stroke ... a mild heart attack? What?"

In the back of my mind there's a niggling thought that I quickly shove down ... then shove down again ... and again. Then, despite my severest attempts to trap it, the thought springs full-blown and scary into my consciousness.

"Could it be God?"

I cringe and duck slightly, batting my hand in front of my face as if whisking off a mosquito. "Hell, no, it couldn't be God! What would God want with *me*? I'm a heathen! I don't go to church! I doubt nearly everything ... especially God! And I take God's name in vain a whole lot! It can't be ... God!"

But the feeling of utter peace stays with me, and I love it, and, in truth, I'm not anxious for it to leave.

When I arrive back at camp, the night is cave-dark, and even the etchings of the trees have disappeared from the horizon. The cook tent glows a pale yellow from a distance, heated by the stove and lighted by the hissing lantern; I can smell dinner cooking from a long way off and hear people inside.

Don and Sue ask if I had any problems.

"Everything was fine," I say.

I tell no one what happened because I don't know what to say ... and because I'm not sure myself. I'm not a talkative person by nature, but that night I'm even quieter.

WRESTLING THE LIGHT

To wrestle with, and for, the light for some meaning in life, is always a way of being in the presence of God.

—*Ted Loder*, Wrestling the Light

After I returned home, I tried to discount the experience time and time again, with little lasting effect. It was just too strong, and the enduring sense of peace too pervasive and too core. As I tried to find ways of explaining what happened that day, I came to think of it as being ambushed by God. Nothing else fit quite so well. It wasn't an ambush in the usual connotation of something violent or sneaky, but more like the story in the Hebrew Bible (the Jewish sacred text—the Old Testament to Christians) where Jacob wrestles with the angel. He was alone at night, having sent his wife and children across the ford at Jabbok, when a man appeared "and wrestled with him until daybreak" (Genesis 32:24). Though Jacob asked, "Please tell me your name," the man never answered. By the end of the encounter, all Jacob could say was, "I have seen God" (32:30).

Had *I* seen God?

The question pushed all my buttons. I'd been an agnostic—maybe an atheist—most of my life, so what was I to do with this ... this spiritual epiphany? For a very long time I'd sneered at God and pitied people who believed in God. Was I now one of *them*? Grudgingly, in small ways, I began to acknowledge my spiritual side. Enough "things" had happened in my life, even before the ambush, to make me think that God *might* exist and might *occasionally* be involved in my life.

I wasn't confident enough to trust this experience completely, but I knew I wanted more, the way a desert flower thirsts for water. I was tired of being spiritually indehiscent, and I found myself wanting to have more frequent experiences of God. So I began to be more formal in my spiritual quest. I went to several men's spiritual weekends but came away humiliated because none of the other men shared any of my doubts, angers, and frustrations. They *knew*—with certainty!—who God was. These men represented everything about organized religion that offends me, and I retreated into my familiar (but now semi-) agnostic hole of safety, temporarily content to be a spiritual hermit again.

Then my wife took me on another weekend, this one for both women and men. Though I was prepared to endure isolation and humiliation again, I went to please my wife. But to my joy, I was surrounded by people who were openly struggling with their spirituality and their relationships to God. This certainly wasn't like the church of my childhood! The church I grew up in was a cure for insomnia, but this experience was meaningful and personal. These people talked about a God who worked in their lives, and was relevant. I was mesmerized.

At Sunday's chapel service, as the first strong sunshine of the weekend flowed through the stained-glass windows and bathed me with warmth and light, I told God I was tired of fighting. At that precise moment, the exact instant the words left my lips, a jolt of electricity blew through my body, set every hair on end, and I experienced the second most soul-deep peace of my life. In the wilderness of my struggle with God, we'd now met on non-ambush terms, and finally my relationship with God seemed to be moving from the wrestling mat to the dance floor. But the dance was just beginning.

For years, despite much professional success, I'd had a growing sense that I wasn't doing what was right for me. Work had become less and less satisfying, and I was becoming less engaged and more depressed because I saw no way out; I had too many years invested, too many skills acquired, and too much money on the line. But if this work of nearly thirty years wasn't what I was meant to do, then what in the world was?

At the same time, parents, aunts, and uncles on all sides of the family began dying with startling rapidity. Several times over this period, I sank into deep depression, and it seemed that God, once again, was at a far distant place. There are many wildernesses besides those of nature, and this was one of them. I hated this wilderness for its persistence and its power over me.

As often happens when people realize through harsh experience how little in life they really control, and they reach a certain level of desperation, they reluctantly turn to God as a last resort. So it was with me. With glacial slowness, I stopped denying that my heart and my truest gifts lay not in business, but in service. At about this time, and on a fairly frequent basis, people—including a former employer—began telling me what a great minister I'd be.

I blanched. "Me? A minister?!" I was horrified, but in a deep secret place that I hardly recognized, I was also intrigued.

Shakespeare wisely observed in *Hamlet* (act 2, scene 2), "There's many a slip 'twixt cup and lip," and that wisdom applied here. In my case, there was an ocean between *admitting* that my heart was in service and *acting* upon it; each time I came close to taking the plunge, I'd step back.

There is an ambush story in the Christian New Testament that occurred shortly after Jesus was crucified and resurrected, about the young man Paul before he became an apostle. His name was Saul then, and he hated and persecuted the "Jesus Followers," as they were called, killing or imprisoning many of them. One day, on his way to Damascus to expose and punish more Jesus Followers, a brilliant light suddenly flashed around him, and a voice asked why he was persecuting those who believed in Jesus. Saul, understandably, fell to the ground and then posed the age-old human question about the Divine, asking, "Who are you?" This is the same question Jacob asked of the "man" he was wrestling, but, unlike Jacob, Saul got an answer: "I am the one you are persecuting" (Acts 9:5). Then the voice told him to get up and go to the city, where he would be told what to do. Imagine what must have been going through Saul's mind. I had a glimmer of how Saul/Paul must have felt; for who was less qualified to be a minister than I?

However, somewhere along my own winding, foot-dragging way, I'd begun to believe that my braided path to belief might enable me to speak with authenticity about spiritual doubts and wrestling with faith. I'd seen God from both sides of belief. I'd ignored God, rejected God, wrestled with God, and finally danced with God. But what church would have me? And, what church would I want? I was too irreverent and had too many doubts about organized religion. With some relief, the poor fit looked like my way out; ministry as I knew it just wasn't going to suit either of us.

But when you're ambushed by God, it's not that easy to ignore.

I was sitting in the local library, wondering how I was going to deal with this insistent impulse for ministry, when I put voice to the question. "What am I going to do with this?" I whispered to the ether.

And the voice of inspiration (God?) answered immediately, something to this effect: "You are an idiot, aren't you? Take people into the wilderness to find what you found!"

There are times in one's life when the world stands still, and pure, slender truth enters the room. This was one of those times. I shot to my feet and shouted "YES!" at the top of my lungs. The librarians shushed "No!" to my shouts, but I walked out of the library knowing that inspiration had just laid out the path for me. I knew instinctively that it fit me better than anything else in the world could, and I did fist pumps all the way to the street.

"I THINK I SAW GOD THIS EVENING!"

What else is nature but God?
—*Seneca the Younger (4 BCE–65 CE),*
Roman philosopher and statesman

So that's why I'm canoeing on the Rio Grande, leading seven travelers on a wilderness journey, looking for God. Ultimately, I left the business world and went to seminary to create a ministry called Renewal in the Wilderness, which takes people from any faith—and frequently none—into the wilderness to seek an intense spiritual connection. Our trips have served Jews, Christians, Buddhists, and agnostics; Anglos, Asians, and African Americans; laypeople, clergy, women, and men. And they come with just as diverse a range of outdoor experience.

On this particular trip, only two of the seven have had any significant wilderness experience, and only one has canoed much. There are some Class II rapids on this part of the Rio—not particularly difficult, but they do grab your attention—so there have been challenges offered and met. The group is feeling very good about what they've done, both physically and spiritually.

And they should. They are pilgrims who have willingly thrown themselves into this environment; they have been tested—and are still being tested—and they have not been found wanting. These are very different people than they were four days ago.

Yesterday was "hump" day, the third day of our sojourn. This is usually the day when most people new to wilderness travel predictably leave behind the "ohmyGodI'minthewilderness!" attitude of breathless panic to add some punctuation and spaces—and some true grace—to restructure that sentence with surprised pleasure: "Oh, my God ... I'm in the wilderness! ... and I'm not just surviving, I'm *thriving*!" They've crossed the threshold.

Each night we come together in a circle to talk about our experiences of the past twenty-four hours. Everyone has stories to tell, but that particular night Frank was breathless, squirming like a kindergartner, and said instantly, almost yelling, *"I think I saw God this evening!"*

He needed no encouragement.

"It was the damndest thing! I was sitting on the bluff wondering if I would ever personally experience God ... thinking it would have to be something big and spectacular, like a burning bush for me to recognize it ... when I heard a whirring sound right down here." He pointed at a particularly beautiful flower on the right side of his Hawaiian shirt, just above his belt.

"It was a *hummingbird*, for God's sake, and it was hovering *right here*!" He continued finger-stabbing at the flower. "It stayed there for about thirty seconds before it flew off, but for thirty seconds this incredible, tiny, iridescent creature and I were ten inches apart, and ..."

His voice trailed off, and he suddenly seemed far away as his face clouded. Very quietly he said, almost in a whisper: "... and how can I say I saw God in that hummingbird?" He looked downriver, then slowly, quizzically back at us: "But how can I say that I didn't?"

"How can I say that I didn't?"

In that one short question Frank summed up why we need to go to the wilderness: We need, truly *need*, to be startled by God in ways that don't seem possible in our civilized lives. This is why people, from ancient times to modern, continue to seek out the wilderness: to leave the everyday, to simplify, to open our lives to the possibility of God's personal interest in us, and to experience the transcendent.

Having said all this—and in spite of believing it to my bones and having had many experiences of God's presence—I'll admit there are still times when I, as a former agnostic, sometimes ask myself, as Frank did, "How can I say I see divinity in the wilderness? How can I say I feel God's presence in a chorus of loons, in the throaty chuffing of a family of otter, in the primal call-and-response howling of wolves, in the splendor of a bald eagle, in a gibbous moon's shimmering wash of orange light on dark moving water, in the healing silence of wild places, or in a day when my soul has known the amazing grace of utter peace for six straight hours? How can I say I see God in those things?"

But, like Frank—and echoing his new wisdom—how can I say that I don't?

QUESTIONS FOR REFLECTION

- Have you ever had an outdoor experience of "Something Bigger than I Am"? What was the setting and how did it affect you?

- In what ways can you identify with the idea of being "ambushed by God"?

- What is your relationship with organized religion?

- What do your religious traditions teach you about wilderness encounters with God?

- In what areas of your life do you have a sense that something is not quite "right"?

- Where do you sense God's presence the most?

- Have you ever felt the desire to seek out something more spiritual in your life? Where can you imagine doing that?

2

It's in Our DNA

The wilderness is an ancient, universal experience.

A UNIVERSAL LANGUAGE

Wilderness is a necessity.... There must be places for human beings to satisfy their souls.

—*John Muir (1838–1914), conservationist and founder of the Sierra Club*

Hanging over my desk is a large color photograph that I took at the beginning of a monthlong backpacking trip in Alaska. The picture is both truly imposing and utterly serene, which in the wilderness is not a contradiction. Whenever my soul needs a lift and I can't be in the real wilderness, I look at this picture.

At the bottom of the photo, in the center, are low Alaskan scrub willows that look almost lime green, the color of budding spring. They're delicate, wispy, and flexible. On either side they're framed by much taller, dark green pine trees standing like guardians, stoic (as they must be when scoured by Alaskan winters) in their erect bearing and close-quarter formation. The pines and willows lead down to the very broad Susitna River, slightly milky-colored because of glacial runoff.

27

Across the river is another forest of boreal pines that follow the riverbank and begin to march to the north in an unbroken phalanx of dark green. Behind those pines is the beginning of the Alaska Range, jagged, brown, and gray, thrust up abruptly from the table-flatness of the Susitna Valley. And jutting from the middle of the Alaska Range, dominating it, rises Mount McKinley—the fabled Denali ("The Great One")—the highest mountain in North America. Measured from its base to the peak, Denali is taller than Mount Everest. Denali is dressed completely in white, like an ermine king, as are its mountains-in-waiting, Mount Foraker and Mount Hunter, on either side. The cloudless azure sky at the top of the photo frames the brilliance and remoteness of Denali, while the living green of the forests at the bottom gives almost understandable proportion to its immensity.

Whenever I look at this picture, my soul seems to grow, and whatever tension I'm experiencing drops away, even if just temporarily. Seeing the photo takes me back there, and I can almost smell the pines, hear the river, and see Denali again. In that moment, I'm renewed.

My reaction to scenes such as this, and scenes of many other natural wildernesses—even if they are just photographs or paintings—is not mine alone. Even my life-bending experience on the dogsled trip wasn't even a little bit unique. I've spent enough time in research and conversation, and on wilderness trips with people from many religious backgrounds, to come to the belief that the ability of a wilderness experience to affect people's spiritual lives is ancient and profound, and it utterly ignores religious and cultural boundaries.

Trip after trip, I see this amazing phenomenon in action. And it has worked this way for thousands of years, across the globe. It seems that we humans find a "face" of divinity—however we define divinity—in the wilderness. If there is a universal understanding of God's presence (or of Something Bigger than Us, if a person doesn't believe in God) that we can all comprehend, it probably is the language we learn in God's wild places: a language of testing, serenity, and peace so timeless that it transcends our theological differences.

Take the following reflections of Mikhail Gorbachev and Martin Luther. The authors could hardly be more different: The former is a twentieth-century atheist (and former chairman of the Soviet Union), and the latter is the fifteenth-century father of Protestantism. Yet, as they talk about how nature touches their souls, they sound quite similar:

> I believe in the cosmos. All of us are linked to the cosmos. Look at the sun: If there is no sun, then we cannot exist. So nature is my god. To me, nature is sacred; trees are my temples and forests are my cathedrals.
>
> —Mikhail Gorbachev

> God writes the Gospel not in the Bible alone, but on the trees and flowers and clouds and stars.
>
> —Martin Luther

Both men are saying that exposure to nature is a way to experience something life-giving and wiser, something bigger, more fertile, and more powerful than we are.

GOD'S CONVERSATION WITH US

> Every natural object is a conductor of divinity.
>
> —John Muir

For eons, the wilderness has been a vehicle for spiritual and personal growth. Over the centuries, regardless of cultures and beliefs, people have turned to nature to find spiritual connection. This impulse, as one of my college professors was fond of saying, is omniscient and omnipresent. Religions across great spans of both time and geography have recognized the wilderness as a place that brings us to a more basic, personal, and dependent relationship with the Divine.

If religion is at least partially defined as a way for people to connect with God, then throughout the world, nature is often seen as a touchstone, a means to that connection. Some religions believe in one God (Judaism, Christianity, Islam); some, in many gods (Shintoism, Hinduism, Taoism); and some, in no god at all (Buddhism). Whatever our religious persuasion, human beings have a spiritual yearning, which seems to be encoded in our DNA, that is often fulfilled through contact with nature.

Most of the world's largest, most influential religions were born in the wilderness, often in the desert. When we consider the desert's utter sparseness, its lack of anything friendly to humans, we can begin to understand why it was the labor room of at least three major religions: Judaism, Christianity, and Islam.

JUDAISM

> The heavens are telling the glory of God and the firmament proclaims God's handiwork.
>
> —*Psalm 19:1*

Although we humans now go to the wilderness to find God, the story of the Hebrew Bible actually begins, in a wonderful reversal, with God finding us in the wilderness. About 4,100 years ago in the Middle East, God began a consistent conversation with people, starting with a man named Abraham. God had spoken to many people before Abraham, but it was with Abraham that God began to form a nation dedicated to worshipping one God. In this seminal story, the usual searcher/searchee positions were reversed, and God was the one who searched out Abraham in the wilderness of Ur, promising him that he would become the father of a great nation.

The wilderness was also a place of testing for Abraham. Abraham's faith in God's power and promise was expressed and re-expressed many times in the wilderness, as God convinced Abraham and his wife, Sarah, both in their seventies, to leave everything they knew and move to a land of strangers. In perhaps the greatest test of faith, God told Abraham to take his only son, Issac, to a mountaintop and sacrifice him. Abraham was prepared to follow through; we can only imagine the anguish he must have been feeling. But just before he drove the knife into his son's chest, God stayed Abraham's arm, saying, "Now I know that you fear God" (Genesis 22:12).

Like the famous statue of the Ideal of Justice, blindfolded to those it served so it served all equally, the wilderness was indiscriminate in its power to change lives, affecting leaders and servants alike. Hagar, an Egyptian slave girl who served Abraham and Sarah, experienced a critical turning point in the wilderness as well. When God first appeared to her in the wilderness to tell her the future of her son, Ishmael (from whose descendents Islam would be founded), she responded with the question that still reverberates for all of us: "Have I really seen God?" (Exodus 16:13). Later, when Sarah banished Hagar and Ishmael back to the wilderness, God appeared to Hagar once again, saying, "Do not be afraid" (Exodus 21:17). This time the message was laden with the peace that many still seek in wilderness settings.

As the events that make up the Hebrew Bible unfolded, God appeared to many people, and those appearances were almost always in the wilderness. The wilderness was not only a crucible of testing and revelation, but also a place of learning, for that is where people realized most truly that they could neither create nor control what surrounded them, and they learned to rely on God.

But the lessons of the wilderness were not easily learned. When God first confronted Moses in the form of a burning bush, in the desert at Mount Horeb, Moses protested his adequacy to meet the challenge God proposed: to lead the Israelites out of captivity in Egypt (Exodus 3:11). The Israelites had their own issues, however. Even after their dramatic rescue from Egyptian slavery, they feared the challenge of the desert more than they feared their bondage. Frightened by the lack of food and water, they complained to Moses, "You have brought us out into this wilderness to kill this whole assembly with hunger" (Exodus 16:3).

Yet the wilderness was also a place where they experienced God's infinite compassion and patience—and love. In the books Exodus through Deuteronomy, the saga of the Israelites' journey through the wilderness often reveals God as wooing the people: "Therefore, behold, I will allure her [Israel], and bring her into the wilderness, and speak tenderly to her" (Hosea 2:14, ESV).

It took forty years of wandering in the wilderness, through many hardships and false steps, before the Israelites could emerge as a people, free, finally, of their slave mentality. As they wandered through the desert, they learned, reluctantly, that the wilderness had much to teach them—mostly through what was *not* there: nothing made by humankind, nothing of comfort, no predictable oases other than God. They began to understand that the "emptiness" of the wilderness could reveal God. Only after the wilderness taught them enough about God, about their reliance on God, and about themselves could they move into their promised future.

In a later Hebrew Bible story, the wilderness became the teacher to the prophet Elijah. Fleeing to evade the wrath of Jezebel, he spent forty days in the wilderness before he finally came to understand God's fullness: "Now there was a great wind ... and after the wind an earthquake ... and after the earthquake a fire ... and after the fire a sheer sound of silence" (1 Kings 19:11b–12). But God was not in the great wind, the earthquake, or the fire, though they came at God's command. Rather, it was only in the great wilderness silence that followed that Elijah could hear the voice of God.

In perhaps one of the best-known stories of the Hebrew Bible, the young shepherd David had a wilderness encounter that changed not only his life but also the course of history. In a valley between two mountains, David took on the feared Philistine champion, the ten-foot-tall Goliath, even though David's king, Saul, had told him, "You are not able to go against this Philistine to fight with him; for you are just a boy." Yet David trusted "the Lord, who saved me from the paw of the lion and from the paw of the bear" to protect him (1 Samuel 17:33, 37), and there began to fulfill God's destiny for him as the greatest king of Israel.

CHRISTIANITY

> Come away to a deserted place all by yourselves and rest
> a while.
>
> —*Jesus, to his disciples (Mark 6:31)*

In the Christian Bible, the New Testament, the record continues of the wilderness moving into people, and people into it. When the angel Gabriel appeared to Mary, telling her that she would be the mother of God's son, the setting was the small town of Nazareth on the edge of the desert.

John the Baptist, who prepared the way for Jesus's ministry, was a wilderness man who conducted his ministry in the honesty of wild places rather than be compromised by the follies and ego-centricities of more civilized settings: "The child grew and became strong in spirit, and he was in the wilderness until the day he appeared publicly to Israel" (Luke 1:80).

Immediately after his baptism by John, Jesus was "driven" into the desert for forty days of temptation and fasting to prepare him for the difficult ministry that lay ahead.[1] After his ministry began, Jesus would retreat often and intentionally to the wilderness: "But now more than ever the word about Jesus spread abroad; many crowds would gather to hear him ... but he would withdraw to deserted places and pray" (Luke 5:16). Jesus knew that only in the emptiness of the wilderness could he be renewed—refilled—in his relationship with God to continue his work.

Likewise, the apostle Paul went to the wilderness of Arabia for (some say) a very lengthy time (Galatians 1:17) after his conversion experience on the road to Damascus (Acts 9:1–9). We can well imagine that it was a time of purging himself of all he'd believed and stood for in his former life as a zealous persecutor of the Jesus Followers, and also a time of opening himself up to the new path God had in mind for him as a disciple of the very man he'd loathed.

ISLAM

> Whithersoever ye turn, there is the presence of Allah.
> —*Qur'an 2:115*

Islam, like Judaism, has a two-edged relationship with the spiritual power of wild places. On one edge, nature is seen as proof of God's existence. But on the other edge, to revere nature beyond its correct proportion is to put it in contention with worshipping God, which is blasphemous. Like Judaism and Christianity, Islam was born in the wilderness: Muslims believe that Muhammad was sitting alone in a cave on Mount Hira, in the wilderness near Mecca, when the angel Gabriel appeared to him and taught him the verses of the Qur'an. Central to the traditional Islamic view is a belief in the oneness of nature and humans, which are both of the same creator. And although humans are God's greatest creation, the Qur'an cautions that "the creation of the heavens and the earth is a greater (matter) than the creation of men: Yet most men understand not" (40:57).

The Qur'an teaches that natural things are *ayat* (signs) pointing to the existence of God:

> We show them our Signs in the (furthest) regions (of the earth) ... until it becomes manifest to them that this is the Truth. (41:53)

> On the earth are signs for those of assured Faith.... Will ye not then see? (51:20–21)

> Do they not look at the Camels, how they are made? And at the Sky, how it is raised high? And at the Mountains, how they are fixed firm? And at the Earth, how it is spread out? (88:17–20)

According to this view, every particle of nature is believed to be living and conscious; nature, like humans, is alive and intelligent. Humans, as part of nature, may commune with all of creation through this consciousness and share its secrets. As the thirteenth-century Sufi poet Rumi described, everything in the universe is "a pitcher brimming with wisdom and beauty."[2] Nature, accordingly, is beautiful because it is infused with the light of God.

EMBEDDED IN OUR DNA

> Heaven is my father and earth is my mother, and even such a small creature as I finds an intimate place in their midst.
> —Chang Tsai (1020–1077 CE), Neoconfucian philosopher

Many other cultures in other times, other religions, and other philosophies also verify how deeply the wilderness is embedded in our DNA. Pilgrims from the Buddhist (India, Tibet, Nepal, China, Japan), Confucian (China), Taoist (China), Hindu (India), Shinto (Japan), Native American (North and South America), and Inuit (Arctic Circle) traditions would recognize and understand the core elements of each other's wilderness traditions and rituals because they have many similarities. In vastly disparate places, each tradition uses the wilderness to rid its pilgrims of the civilized baggage they carry, and to take them to a deeper, more authentic spiritual place.

BUDDHISM

> Seeking the supreme state of sublime peace, I wandered ... until ... I saw a delightful stretch of land and a lovely woodland grove, and a clear flowing river with a delightful forest so I sat down thinking, "Indeed, this is an appropriate place to strive for the ultimate realization of ... *nirvana*."
>
> —Buddha (563–483 BCE)

The Buddha was born Siddhartha Gautama in the mountains of Northern India. His father, a rich and powerful ruler, tried to shield Siddhartha from knowledge of worldly decay, death, sickness, and unhappiness. But when Siddhartha discovered that the world was, indeed, filled with pain, he abandoned his privileged life to learn why suffering existed and to search for perfect enlightenment. Finally, after years of searching, he sat in a forest under a Bodhi tree until he attained nirvana (in Sanskrit, "the highest happiness," which is attained when all of the passions are purged). In the serenity of nature, absent the striving and ego involvement characteristic of the civilized world, Siddhartha found the way of enlightenment and became Buddha ("the Enlightened"). To this day, most Buddhist monasteries or retreat centers are located in forests.

While it remains an open question as to whether Buddhism is a religion or a philosophy, in the spiritual peace it brings its followers there can be no doubt. As the ninth-century Chinese Buddhist poet and layman Han-shan wrote, "Here in the wilderness I am completely free."[3]

CONFUCIANISM

> The man of wisdom delights in water; the man of
> humanity delights in mountains.
>
> —*Confucius*, Analects 6:21

During the time that the Buddha lived and worked—around 600
BCE—Confucianism began in China with the famous philosopher
Confucius. Confucians believe that nature is inherently moral,
and therefore people are encouraged to seek self-realization in harmony with nature. Although earlier Western culture has looked at
Confucianism as an agrarian philosophy, it is now viewed as a
complex and rich religious system that affirms the relationship
between people and the natural world. For Confucians, nature
embodies the best standard for all things and is the basis of a stable, healthy society.

TAOISM

> From wonder into wonder existence opens.
>
> —*Lao-tzu, sixth-century BCE Chinese philosopher and*
> *traditional author of the Tao Te Ching*

Taoism (or Daoism) means "The Way," which is shorthand for
"the way of nature." Begun in China around the same time as
Confucianism (and Buddhism in India), Taoism views the natural
world as a place with the capacity for self-transcendence; it can,
therefore, be both religious and natural. The belief system of
Taoism might be condensed into two words: "Follow nature." In
other words, we should, like water, flow downhill and seek our natural course in life, not fighting against its obstacles but flowing
around them.

Taoists believe that, because the natural world is always
changing, humans cannot keep abreast of the changes, and for
that reason we should respect nature's ability to transform. Early

Tao religious centers were located on mountains or in other wild areas that served as sacred places and refuges where ordinary humans could transcend their own nature and find a way to attain the celestial life.

HINDUISM

> May there be peace in the skies, peace in the atmosphere, peace on earth, peace in the waters. May the healing plants and trees bring peace; may there be peace [on and from] the world, the deity.
> —*Veda (Hindu) hymn, more than 3,000 years old*

Followers of Hinduism, which gets its name from the Sindhu River, are taught to live in harmony with nature and recognize that divinity is reflected in all living things, including plants and animals. The *rishis* (spiritual leaders) of the past had a great respect for nature. They perceived that all physical things are a shadow of the spiritual, culminating in the greeting of *namaste*, which means "I recognize and salute the Divine within you."

SHINTOISM

> Even in a single leaf of a tree, or a tender blade of grass, the awe-inspiring Deity manifests itself.
> —*Urabe-no-Kanekuni (ca. 720 CE), Shinto poet*

Shinto (Way of the Gods) is Japan's indigenous religion and dates back to the fifth or sixth century CE. Shintoism is polytheistic, and its gods (*kami*) range from the very powerful to the very humble. Worship is often directed at natural forms (mountains, trees, rocks, streams, and other elements of nature)—but particularly at forests—and is driven by a great reverence and love for nature. Shintoism is, in fact, primarily the worship of nature. It teaches that we can find spiritual fulfillment through exposure to the natural world.

NATIVE AMERICAN

> We should know that all things are the works of the Great Spirit. We should know that He is within all things: the trees, the grasses, the rivers, the mountains, and all the four-legged animals, and the winged peoples; and even more important, we should understand that He is also above these things and peoples.[4]
>
> —*Black Elk (ca. 1863–1950), Lakota shaman*

North American Indian tribes were very widely dispersed and so had a variety of spiritual beliefs. Some tribes were monotheistic and some were polytheistic, but in one way or another they each exhibited great respect, if not reverence, for all the natural things that surrounded them and influenced their lives. In most tribes there was no word for religion, for their everyday lives were so tightly intertwined with their spiritual lives that they found it inconceivable to think of them separately.

They knew that their existence depended on what nature would provide them, so they would ask the animals they hunted to allow the Indians to kill them so the humans might eat. Once the animal was killed, the hunters would give thanks to its spirit for its sacrifice. Out of respect, and a belief that all lives in the world are interlaced, the Indians rarely killed more than they needed. Their ethic of treating the earth with respect followed the same pattern. They believed that all elements of the natural world—including animals, plants, earth, rocks—had a unique intelligence. They saw no superiority of one species over the other, for everything and everyone fit into *Wakan-Tanka's* (the Great Spirit) plan.

South American Indians, as exemplified by the Quechua tribes (which include the Inca), were polytheistic and pantheistic (that is, God is everything, and everything is God), and believed, as did the North American Indians, that nature was the bearer of the divine. Many of the Andean mountain areas were considered sacred, and still are today. From my backpacking trip in the Peruvian Andes, I can attest to the overarching sense of divine presence in those mountains. They're often fog-enshrouded, they're lushly green, they're rugged and filled with waterfalls and tumbling creeks. They're intensely spiritual places.

INUIT

> The arch of sky and mightiness of storms
> Have moved the spirit within me,
> Till I am carried away
> Trembling with joy.
> —*Uvavnuk, twentieth-century Inuit shaman*

Like the American Indians, the Inuit in the Arctic coastal areas of Alaska, Siberia, the Northwest Territories of Canada, Nunavut, Labrador, and Greenland believe that all animals possess souls, and therefore the hunters pay great respect to the animals they kill, sometimes performing rituals that allow the animals' souls to return to their place of origin. The Inuit have a vision quest tradition that uses the extreme forces of nature to shape the spiritual lives of the young men in their small ice-bound communities. A shaman named Igjugarjuk said:

> All true wisdom is only to be learned far from the dwellings of men, out in the great solitudes, and is only to be attained through suffering. Privation and suffering are the only things that can open the mind of man to those things which are hidden from others.[5]

DEEP CALLS TO DEEP

If you are searching for a Neter *[a god], observe Nature!*
—Proverb inscribed on Egypt's Temple of Karnak
(ca. 1400 BCE)

There is an impulse so primal, so deeply embedded in our collective subconscious, that it goes back to the near beginnings of civilization. It is a hunger for something more connected, more vital, and deeper than we are; it is a hunger almost never satisfied in civilized places.

I see this hunger often when I give presentations about Renewal in the Wilderness trips. At the end of virtually every talk, people approach me with eyes that are bright with reminiscence. They tell me stories of how alive they felt in their childhood when they were outside in nature, often on camping trips. Then they say they'd love to take one of my trips, but add, "Now [and this is predictable] my idea of roughing it is staying at the Holiday Inn." Their hunger for a deeper spiritual connection is written on their faces and in the wistfulness of their eyes; it's written in their body language, in the hesitant way they leave our conversations. In a layer just below the surface of their rationality, they recognize their hunger or they would have avoided contact with me altogether. Yet, they can't bridge the gap of leaving the comfortable for the less comfortable, leaving the known for the unknown, leaving the "safety" of civilization for what they perceive to be the hazards of the wilderness. And in doing that, they resign themselves to a life that is less rich than it could be. Their eyes dim a bit with resignation as they walk away, thinking they've made the "adult," "rational" decision.

But what about a spiritual quest is rational?

In an attempt to have an answer for that polite Holiday Inn excuse, I once conducted a nonscientific study of artwork on the covers of books about spiritual renewal, spiritual healing, or

41

contemplation. I found that, although less than 2 percent of the books were actually about going to the wilderness to find God, about 85 percent of them had wilderness scenes on the covers ... not unlike this one.

There's a reason for the scenes of nature on all these books: The wilderness is imprinted on us, and we respond to it! When we imagine places where we might come in contact with the holy, we imagine a wild, natural scene. Even looking at photographs of these places brings feelings of peace. Not surprisingly, a study showed that patients who could see a natural vista—mountain, forest, or landscape—from their hospital beds recovered faster than patients whose view was limited to urban vistas. Also, not surprisingly, kids with attention deficit disorder (ADD) learn better when they're exposed to some of nature's visual and experiential bounty.[6]

Actually *being* in a natural setting is even better than looking at pictures of it—infinitely better—because we are immersed in it, we wrap it around us; we feel and hear its breezes, smell and touch the trees, flowers, and earth; we hear and see the animals. We are active participants rather than passive observers.

When the early Desert Fathers and Mothers of the third, fourth, and fifth centuries wanted to live a more God-centered life than city living allowed them, they retreated to the deserts of the Middle East:

> Abba Ammoun ... came to Clysma one day to meet Abba Sisoes. Seeing that Abba Sisoes was grieved because he had left the desert, Abba Ammoun said to him, "Abba, why grieve about it? What would you do in the desert, now you are so old?"
>
> The old man ... said to him, "What are you saying to me ... ? Was not the mere liberty of my soul enough?"[7]

"The liberty of my soul." To be in a wild place is to feel that liberty of the soul. When people describe their experiences in the wilder-

ness, they use words such as peaceful, uninhibited, in tune, whole, infinite, small, refreshed, joyful, enraptured. These are all words of health and connection—physical, spiritual, emotional—and they come from the very deep place of our genetic link with the natural world. Our impulse—yours and mine—to go to natural places to be in the presence of the Divine is ancient and widespread, and buried very deeply within us.

Just as our spiritual forebears did, we go to the wilderness to find a more authentic spiritual experience than civilization usually allows. The wilderness opens us to God's presence because it reduces everything to what is exactly necessary, and no more. In places like that we more genuinely feel a need for God, and sense that God is near at hand. One writer expressed her wilderness experience in these words:

> I remember the way the moon rose up over the canyon wall and then cast shadows over the entire canyon floor. I loved just lying there and staring up at the stars ... and being filled with this sense of infinitude.... I felt a complete merging with the surrounding environment. Instead of sitting back and observing it, it's like I was moving into it ... or rather it was moving into me.[8]

Being in the natural world has worked for millennia to bring spiritual wholeness to people on all parts of the earth, to create a sense of wonder, and to give us a knowledge of things larger, more wonderful, and more permanent than ourselves. What we humans build can be beautiful and inspirational, though even at its best, it is intrusive, artificial, and, ultimately, temporary. But in wild places there is a flowing and natural grace, an innate recognition of the timelessness of God.

As poet Joyce Kilmer said in his poem *Trees*, published in 1919, "Only God can make a tree." His words could easily include all elements of the natural world—all its plants and animals, and its natural features. In wild places, even if we cannot see the actual face of God, we can at least look at God's natural creation—God's first and truest place of worship—and know we are as close to God's presence as it is possible to be in this life. The authors of spiritual renewal books know this; so do you and I. There is something genetic about the sense of connection with the Divine through wild and beautiful places.

> For one week, the world seemed perfect. We lived in the present, completely focused on the demands of the trip. We were a group of the faithful and the questioning ... Christian and Jewish ... clergy and laity ... men and a woman, in their mid-fifties to early seventies in varying degrees of fitness ... who were canoeing in the Minnesota Boundary Waters.... Personal theology never dominated our conversations because we realized that we were all there for the same thing, however we sought it.
>
> It was personal revelations that were so memorable. A poem dashed off during a journal-writing period left us impressed and moved. One person's unabashed dialogue with God was countered with another person's "I don't think in those terms," yet the group seemed comfortable with both. What a perfect setting to bring people together with different faiths; the wilderness showed us how similar our spiritual experiences are despite our religious differences.
>
> —Don Rubovits, on a canoe trip
> in the Boundary Waters Canoe Area

Carl Jung, the famous Swiss psychologist, said that the world has a collective unconscious that contains the wisdom and knowledge of the fullness of human history. According to Jung's theory, none of the knowledge of creation is lost. It is there to be tapped, if we have the sensitivity. The same is true, I believe, of our collective *spiritual* unconscious: The impulse to see and be in natural settings when we want to be in communion with God is elementally powerful, elementally within us. Deep calls to deep, and it is in the embrace of the wilderness that our deepest yearnings can be answered.

QUESTIONS FOR REFLECTION

- Look around your home or workplace for pictures or symbols of nature. What longings do they touch in you?

- Think of a story from your religious tradition (or a tradition with which you are familiar) about someone encountering God in the wilderness. What connection(s) does this experience have with your own life?

- Are there any spiritual ideas about, or approaches to, nature that you would like to explore further? What are they? How might you begin?

- When you think about the wilderness, what "Holiday Inn excuses" of your own come to mind? How might you respond to them in light of this chapter's reading?

- What longing (spoken or unspoken) do you sense about the idea of "going into the wilderness" to connect with the Divine?

- What "wildernesses" are accessible to you? You don't need thousands of miles of open space and a backpack or canoe to move into a natural setting. Think local parks, state parks, rivers, ponds, or lakes. Where might you go this week? How might you prepare spiritually for the experience?

3

PRESENCE IN THE PRESENT
THE WILDERNESS BRINGS US INTO THE PRESENT MOMENT, INTO GOD'S PRESENCE.

AN EXCELLENT TEACHER

Earth and sky, woods and fields, lakes and rivers,
the mountain and the sea, are excellent schoolmasters,
and teach some of us more than we can ever learn from books.
—*Sir John Lubbock (1834–1913), English naturalist*

We've been paddling hard for the past three days—not that we've traveled so far, but the wind is ferocious. Maddeningly, it seems to be in our faces almost all of the time, in spite of our twisty route through the narrow, serpentine rivers and small lakes of the Boundary Waters Canoe Area of northern Minnesota.

We begin to think there should be some kind of Murphy's Law about the wind always being in our face, so we create our own. One of our group remembers enough high school Latin to dub our law *Ventus Facies*, or "Wind in Our Face," and we yell "*Ventus Facies*" whenever we are assaulted by another rolling boulder of wind that hits our ears with an audible "boom." It becomes both our rallying cry and our response to what nature is testing us with.

Sometimes the wind blows so hard that the water—even as narrow as the rivers and lakes are—has whitecaps. On the rare occasions when there are broadside blasts, they're so potent we're afraid we'll capsize. When we get hit from the side, we hunker down in the canoes to create as low a profile as possible, getting our shoulders as close to gunwale level as is physically do-able. When we can, we grab onto the wild rice or bank grass for some stability, "any anchor in the storm," as the saying goes. But we aren't in a storm—just wind that pummels us like an invisible boxer, with a lot of jabs and, sometimes, huge roundhouse clouts of solid air. We are becoming adept at guessing when the next gusts will slam us because we can usually hear them bursting through the tops of the trees. And we are discovering how to canoe between the holes in the wind.

"*Ventus Facies!*"

As strange as it sounds, we're having fun. Once we learn that we can handle these conditions, that we can travel through the holes, it becomes a challenge we can deal with.

None of us had anticipated that we'd encounter conditions like this in the middle of August, with temperatures that could give us snow! The weather conditions demand—as the wilderness always demands—our complete attention to the present: learning, practicing, and mastering new skills; staying upright, staying warm, staying dry; working with a partner to paddle a canoe efficiently and in a straight line. It all requires intense focus on very present issues. At almost no point since the trip began has any of us spent any meaningful time thinking about the future or the past. We are learning one of the most important lessons the wilderness has to teach us: *Being in the present is crucial.*

A wilderness experience is such an effective teacher because it engages all of our senses—mental, physical, emotional, and spiritual—and focuses them on the same point: the present moment. This is especially important to our spiritual quest because the present is the only time in which we can be aware of God's presence. If our minds and hearts are not fully engaged in the moment—if we're focused on the past or on the future, as we so often are—God's presence can pass us by. As Goethe said, "The present is a powerful deity," and it is the only time we have in which God can intersect with us.

CARPE DIEM

The secret of health for both mind and body is not to mourn for the past, nor to worry about the future, but to live the present moment wisely and earnestly.

—*Buddha (563–483 BCE)*

Being present to be in God's presence is far from a new concept. Horace, the Roman poet, talked about it around 46 BCE, when he said, "In the moment of our talking, envious time has ebbed away. Seize the present." (*"Carpe diem"* is actually what he said, and "seize the day" is how we most often hear it translated.)

The Bible certainly talks of it: For example, in 1 Kings 19:11, God says to Elijah, "Go out and stand on the mountain in the presence of the Lord, for the Lord is about to pass by." Most of us would be fully invested in the moment if we knew that God were about to pass by!

American Indian Plains tribes lived in constant awareness of the possibility of the Divine in the mundane. If they did not live in the moment, they might miss what their *manido*, or guardian spirit, would impart to them, and their lives would be unfulfilled.

John Calvin, the sixteenth-century French lawyer who became a staunch pillar of Protestantism, said:

The reason why the author of the Letter to the Hebrews elegantly calls the universe the appearance of things invisible (Hebrews 11:3) is that this skillful ordering of the universe is for us a sort of mirror in which we can contemplate God, who is otherwise invisible.

The reason why the prophet attributes to the heavenly creatures a language known to every nation (Psalm 19:2ff.) [i.e., "the heavens" and "the firmament," Psalm 19:1] is that therein lies an attestation of divinity so apparent that it ought not to escape the gaze of even the most stupid tribe.

The apostle [Paul] declares this more clearly: "What men need to know concerning God has been disclosed to them ... for one and all gaze upon his invisible nature, known from the creation of the world, even unto his eternal power and divinity" (Romans 1:19–20).

Wherever you cast your eyes, there is no spot in the universe wherein you cannot discern at least some sparks of his glory. You cannot in one glance survey this most vast and beautiful system of the universe, in its wide expanse, without being completely overwhelmed by the boundless force of its brightness.[1]

Implicit in Calvin's statement is the idea that if we are present—as time in nature shows us how to be and demands that we be—then we will be more aware of God's presence. If we are open to the moment, the force of the natural world compels us to become intensely committed to the present, so we can see God.

BE HERE NOW

> The moment one gives close attention to any thing, even a blade of grass, it becomes a mysterious, awesome, indescribably magnificent world in itself.
> —*Henry Miller (1891–1980), American writer*

In the early seventies, Ram Dass wrote a classic book on spirituality that introduced a whole generation of westerners to the teachings of the East. The book was titled *Be Here Now*. Today this phrase, almost more than any other, captures the essence of what "being present" means. Wilderness instructors of Outward Bound–style programs use this as one of the basic rules for the people in their charge (although the wording may be different). As Blair Bertrand and Peter T. Hazelrigg, former Outward Bound instructors who are now ministers, put it:

> Be Here Now. In saying this we mean that all of the distractions, the idols and Egypts we are leaving [reference to the Israelite slaves leaving Egypt with Moses], keep us from being present with God and with each other. To Be Here Now means to forget the TV, the Internet, the CD players, etc., all of those things which make us feel secure, in order that we might risk being truly present to each other. At an even deeper level, Be Here Now means to let go of old routines and ways of living in order that we might learn new routines that will bring life in our new setting, both the wilderness and our transformed everyday life.[2]

At the beginning of each Renewal in the Wilderness trip, I talk with the group about the astounding ability of the wilderness to keep us constantly aware. I tell the new voyageurs that they'll find themselves—body and soul—completely in the present for almost the entire trip. Everything we do is intended to keep them open to everything around them so that they can be completely receptive to however God is present. The wilderness is often the yeast—the catalyst—that allows this to happen.

Each morning we prepare ourselves to be open to the day. We start with meditation exercises that focus on breathing or on being aware of all that's going on around us. We try, with exquisite sensitivity, to be present to the touch and sound and sensation of everything—feeling the air, hearing the wind, listening to the animals, smelling earth's perfumes, being consciously aware of our natural senses. We want to miss nothing. We want to gather it all in like one of those huge parabolic dishes astronomers use to listen to the sounds of the ancient universe, so we train our minds to be present and not run rampant with thoughts of the past or future.

At this moment, though, there's no need to remind this particular Boundary Waters group to be completely in the present because we're being broadsided by more big-wind artillery from the west, just as we locate the beginning of our next portage.

"*Ventus Facies!*" we yell in defiance.

It just feels good to shake our vocal fists, though we're keenly aware that that's the only "control" over the weather we have. Then we pull up our canoes, knowing that we're about to enter the portage from hell. Everyone has been thinking about this since last night, some dreading it.

To its credit, the group has done so well, in spite of the conditions, that we've decided to tackle the hardest route, which includes the portage from the North Kawishiwi River to Greenstone Lake. It's 214 rods in length (a rod is one canoe length, about seventeen feet, so this portage is nearly three-quarters of a mile long). The distance alone is challenging, but our topographical map—which shows hills, valleys, and elevation gain and loss—indicates that this portage is going to be particularly roller-coastery with a lot of hard-rock trail.

People are concerned—we're mostly couch potatoes—but as people do when confronted with hard tasks, we break it into small, definable, manageable pieces, and "gird our loins," as the Bible puts it. We are very much in the present, thinking only of the immediate needs. We eat some gorp for energy, drink a lot of water so we don't "bonk" due to dehydration, and discuss how we're going to handle this long, tough portage. We've done many shorter portages, so we all know our jobs; we're just moving to the varsity team with this one. We lace our boots tightly and start out.

Those who can, shoulder the canoes and start off with their paddle partners ("spotters") walking behind them to offer assistance and warn them about footing conditions and overhanging branches as necessary. Although it would be more efficient for the spotters to also carry packs, we decide that in the interest of safety, the spotters will concentrate only on the carrier, then go back to get a pack at a rest stop.

The system works well. The canoe carriers walk until they get tired, then the spotters help lower the canoe to the ground and go back for a pack while the carriers rest. At some point the spotters and carriers switch places so that all have the experience of both jobs.

The first part of the trail seems as if it's almost straight up; the distance is about an eighth of a mile, but it feels much longer. It's so narrow, rocky, and overgrown that not many people endeavor this portage—and we're learning why. The path is so steep that the carriers have to tilt the front of the canoe upward so it doesn't dig into the trail. Then, across the top of the hill, some parts of the trail are giant-step descents—maybe three or four feet down—between truck-sized boulders so the canoes must be balanced delicately and tilted up or down according to the terrain, so that the front or the back of the boat doesn't smash into the rocks and throw the carrier off balance.

Although the load is unwieldy, and course changes come slowly, it's nevertheless fairly precise work. It's both awkward and delicate, and it has a certain ponderous grace, like elephants doing ballet. Peoples' attention is riveted on the trail, on the task, on the load.

There is an old Chinese proverb that says, "Man who says it cannot be done should not interrupt man doing it." That *amply* describes this group!

No one is thinking about their meetings next week, or their triumphs or failures of last week. We are focused 100 percent on the moment, on each step, on helping each other. People—complete strangers just days ago—have come to know each other in a depth and in a way that they will know few other people—or be known—in their lives. The wilderness doesn't reward pretense, or anything other than complete investment.

We've gotten spread out over the trail, so at about the midpoint of the portage, we regather as a group to rest, to eat more gorp and drink more water, to check in, and to take our collective pulse. Don, a mostly agnostic Jewish layman, and Wesley, a Christian pastor—the two oldest people on the trip—share with us the chant they've composed to bolster each other over the most challenging parts of the trail: "Take your time, put one foot in front of the other, and rest when you must." It's a good chant, and an excellent wisdom, we say—one we could use in every part of our lives. They smile; they're sitting in the middle of the trail, each with one arm over the other's shoulder, looking radiant; they're tired, but obviously pleased with what they've done. Neither is thinking about what's waiting for them back home in their respective business and church. Both are filled with the spiritual experience of watching each other's back.

The taking-care-of-each-other aspect of the portage—checking the trail, warning of obstacles, asking "how're you doing?"—is a very gratifying connection, especially in this do-it-yourself world. Concern for the welfare of others is a physical, in-the-moment reflection of God-in-us. Most religious traditions emphasize the idea that, if we're present to each other, we're present to God. Jesus told his disciples, "Truly I tell you, just as you did it to one of the least of these ... you did it to me" (Matthew 25:40). Abdu'l Baha, a noted nineteenth- and twentieth-century Bahá'í leader, said, "Service to humanity is service to God." Genesis says that we are all created in God's image (1:27); so in helping others, we are, by inference, doing God's work.

After Don and Wesley recite their chant, the group is quiet, and in the silence we realize for the first time since we began the portage that we are nicely protected from the wind by the hills and trees. The air is almost calm where we're sitting, and without the wind, it's much warmer. One of the women, Susan, who's been uncharacteristically silent since we regrouped, says quietly, "I think this is the hardest thing I've ever done ... and I think I'm having the best time of my life."

Her eyes begin to well. She has our attention and, based on the nodding heads, our agreement.

"I'm feeling closer to myself ... more in tune with who I am deep inside ... and certainly closer to God," she says, sweeping her arm in front of her to encompass all the wilderness she can see. "I mean, how could you not feel close to God in a setting like this?"

Everyone is quiet for a while, thinking about Susan's words, and what lies behind them. The wind has momentarily let up, so the woods seem abnormally quiet, as if they're listening for what we'll say next. The sun has broken out, and the shadows cast by the leaves make wavering polka dots on everything.

"Now that I think about it," Wesley says, finally breaking the silence, "I'm pretty darned content. I just realized that, after you started talking, Susan. Maybe it's because of the challenges I've been working through. I can feel myself in the presence of God, like you said. I don't face these kinds of challenges in my ordinary life, so I'm being pushed in ways that are making me see life differently. This whole wilderness thing is helping me experience life much more vividly."

He pauses, shrugs, and smiles. "Of course, we still have to finish this portage, do the solo, then come over this same trail to get back...."

The group laughs. But I think many of us share a similar thought: "If I can do *this*, then I can certainly face the problems back home. I wasn't sure I was up to this trip or that I would have the endurance, but now I know I do. This is something I can take back with me to use when the world seems to close in on me."

The wilderness has expanded our definition of what we're capable of doing and our expectation of how God can present God's presence to us.

SACRED SPACE

> You might think, after many years of teaching a class called "Nature Writers," that I would know what nature meant, but I do not.... The word comes from the Latin, *to be born.*
>
> —*John Hay, twentieth-century nature writer [italics added]*

Once again, our group has had to learn a bit more about the challenges of leaving comfort zones. I think of the term *dehabituating.* Essentially, the idea is that we have to let go of our normal "security blankets," leave our "comfort zone and move to a more effective place of learning which is challenge."[3] So it is with us. We've gotten a bit comfortable during our break, but we still have the second half of the portage to go, and the canoes and packs haven't gotten lighter. After more heartfelt discussion about what this experience is meaning—which makes my own heart sing, because this group's experiences of wilderness spirituality have been my experiences as well—it's time to move on.

We hoist the loads and set off again, carrier and spotter. Fortunately, the second half is much easier than the first—and downhill. The portage trail leads to a beautiful and narrow rocky inlet that looks out on a pristine lake dotted with postcard islands, none of which, unfortunately, is big enough for our group, so we head for a mainland campsite. For whatever reason, the wind has almost completely spent itself, and we canoe across a mirror-topped lake, making the only ripples in the water.

We find a perfect wooded point of land that has a stunning view of the lake from three sides, and we set up camp quickly and efficiently, as if we've done it for a long time. We gather wood, set the fire for cooking, and as the sun begins its slow descent to the horizon and the light edges into evening gold, we find separate rocks on the shore to begin our nightly ritual of foot washing. This is a practical thing, not a religious thing, and yet very sacred, as one of our group reflected:

> *During travel days, our rest stops and portages meant walking in water between canoe and rocky shore. Boots were essential to protect the feet. Because the boots would stay wet all day, we had a dry pair for camp. Each day, once we had set up a new campsite in late afternoon, the foot-washing ritual would begin. Its purpose was to prevent the possibility of foot fungus by having feet that were wet for too long.*
>
> *We would pick out our own private rock along the shore. Sitting on it, we would carefully wash our wet boots, socks and feet (our own), and then wait for the feet to dry. It was a quiet ritual with very little talking. No one wanted to break the spell that comes from taking care of a tired body in such natural beauty. Our rock was our personal zone of contemplation as we thought through the day and took in what lay before us. It was rhythmic and methodical, and even sacred in its own way. Afterward, putting on the dry socks and boots felt wonderful!*
>
> —Don Rubovits, on a canoe trip
> in the Boundary Waters Canoe Area

At dinner that night, and around the campfire afterward, we talk about what has happened during the day, and on the trip so far, especially about how the experience has so effectively kept us connected to the present. Today we've encountered what psychologists call "peak" and "flow" experiences, moments where we lose our sense of self and become "totally immersed in the present moment."[4] These experiences put us in an extreme state of consciousness and heightened sensory awareness that focus us, as a magnifying glass focuses sunlight, on that precise moment to the exclusion of everything else. These moments are most often described as spiritual experiences because they take us to places within our being that we seldom visit.

Everyone, including our Outward Bound instructors, is feeling luxuriantly tired, and accomplished. It's dark now, and the campfire pops and rattles and casts its waving light on us all, creating deep shadows behind us. A pack of wolves begins to howl, and it's so primal that we all catch our breath and look around at each other, eyes wide and thrilled. Susan mouths the word "WOW!" and we nod our heads. It's beautiful and eerie and raises the hair on our arms; it takes us back to long-forgotten moments of childhood wonder when everything astonishes us, and everything is mysterious. We feel very insular, very isolated, and it's a perfect end to a hard but immensely satisfying day. We have been very present to each other, to ourselves, to the moment, and to God. We've each seen the Divine in small things, and we feel grateful, peaceful.

That night we sleep deeply.

The next morning is crystalline. If we could gently flick the edge of it with a fingernail, the morning would chime like a fine goblet. It's Sunday, and people are still feeling as they did when they went to bed: timeless, peace-filled—and a bit sore.

After breakfast, we hold a short interdenominational worship service in which we all participate. As we sit in an extended moment of silent contemplation, a tribe of loons flies nearby, warbling their haunting cry.

I think very often of those loons, who just at the right moment, flew
past us to join us in worship, reminding us of God's presence and
… the need to stay present so we can appreciate those small things.

Those two whole days on Greenstone Lake were just about perfect. I don't mean to go on about the challenges I faced, but they changed the way I can look at my life. I will ever keep that experience with me, and I know I will refer to the challenges when life challenges me. I have my jackpine cone [a pinecone that opens only under the extreme heat of a forest fire to expel its seed—certainly a powerful metaphor of its own] where I can see it often as a reminder that God brought me through those physical challenges and will not leave me now.

—Rev. Wesley Cobbs, on a canoe trip
in the Boundary Waters Canoe Area

Given enough time, the wilderness pries open nearly all its visitors to *feeling* (as well as *seeing*) the spiritual power of their surroundings—and it is rarely a neutral experience. When we are in the wilderness for a length of time—actually part of it, rather than looking at it from a porch or through a window—we put it on and we wear it. It moves with us and we with it; in the Zen sense, we become one. In the unfamiliar wilderness environment, we are very much aware of nearly everything because of its newness. And it is at these times, when we're so totally in the present, that we're most open to the presence of God.

QUESTIONS FOR REFLECTION

On our Renewal in the Wilderness trips, we start each day with a breathing exercise and a Question of the Day. These are not theological questions, but rather personal relationship questions about us and God, questions to help us think about God at ground level and be more open to God's subtleties during the day.

For the next week, give yourself some time each day to "practice the presence," as Brother Lawrence so profoundly taught in his seventeenth-century classic work, *The Practice of the Presence of God*. If you have the opportunity to go to a natural, outdoor setting to reflect, all the better, but a quiet spot in your home or garden will do. The important thing is to be in a place where you won't be interrupted for at least thirty minutes or so, in order to stay focused on the breathing exercise and question, and any thoughts or feelings that arise for you.

Start by getting in a comfortable sitting position, then take three slow and deep cleansing breaths, holding the air in your lungs on the inhale until you need to exhale. (If you've never tried this before, I think you'll be amazed at how calming it is, and how tension drains from your body. I carry my tension in my shoulders and stomach, and I often focus on relaxing both before I begin my meditation exercises.)

If you can, do the breathing exercises first thing in the morning, before you begin your day. Let the Question of the Day simmer on the back burner while you go about your activities. In the evening, come back to the question and reflect or journal about your thoughts and feelings.

Day One: The key to being "present" is to be focused on the present. Begin with deep, cleansing breaths to clear your mind. A focusing word or short saying can help you *not* think of other things, which your mind will be prone to do. For example, silently say the phrase "be here" as you inhale, and "now" as you exhale. It's a great reminder of why you're doing this. Center your awareness on your breathing as you slowly take in each breath and let it out. Be conscious only of that. If you find your mind wandering—and it almost certainly will— bring it back, forgivingly, to your breathing and continue with your "be here/now" chant.

Question of the Day: What is your concept of God?

Day Two: Start this breathing exercise with a slow inhalation and exhalation. Focus on how your lungs feel as the air enters and leaves your body. Be conscious of how your chest rises and falls as you breathe, and of the sense of renewal and hopefulness that accompanies every inhale. If you find your mind wandering, bring it back to your breathing and continue with a "be here/now" chant.

Question of the Day: How would you describe your relationship with God?

Day Three: In today's breathing exercise, focus on how the air cools the edges of your nostrils when you breathe in, and then warms your nostrils as you breathe out. Scan your body for tension and will it away as you focus on the sensation of the air on your nostrils.

Question of the Day: What would you like your relationship with God to be?

Day Four: The ancient Hebrews believed that each breath they took was a gift from God, and that it was, in fact, God's breath. Today, as you breathe in and out, imagine that God's face is close to yours and that you are breathing God's breath. An appropriate chant here is "thank you" on the inhale, and "God" on the exhale. This may be a difficult exercise at first, sensing that God's face is next to yours and you're breathing God's breath, but as you relax into it, it will become much easier and give you a warm sense of God's presence ... a reward for your presence.

Question of the Day: What color do you associate with God? What does that mean for you?

Day Five: On our wilderness trips, we try to extend the rhythmic nature and spirituality of our breathing exercises to our paddling. When we're on flat water, and the elements don't require our constant attention, I encourage people to get into a paddling rhythm and begin to chant, silently or with their partner, something like "thank you" on one stroke and "God" on the next, repeating the words to the rhythm of the strokes. (Meister Eckhart, the medieval Christian mystic, said, "If the only prayer you ever uttered was 'thank you,' that would suffice.") This kind of rhythmic chant is both a prayer and a way to be more keenly aware in the present moment. Today as you do your breathing exercises, practice a silent chant that fits one of your day's ordinary activities. Then, during the day, be aware of your ordinary tasks, particularly any of them that are fairly repetitive, and use this chant to help you re-center.

Question of the Day: What color would you *like* to associate with God? What does *that* mean for you?

Day Six: As on the other days, do some deep-breathing exercise and relax your normal areas of tension. Then choose one small area of your face, such as your forehead or cheek or chin, and try to pick up every sensation you can in that specific area. Initially, the spot you pick may seem to be without any sensation, but stick with it. If that area is still without sensation after a minute or two, go back to your breathing for a while, then return the focus to your face. Other sensations may sprout up around the area you've chosen, so be aware of the type of sensations that emerge. Close your breathing exercise with the "be here/now" chant.

Question of the Day: What do you, personally, want from God? (Think of something specifically for you, not "world peace" or anything general or anything dedicated to another person. This is *your* relationship with God; make it personal.)

Day Seven: Today, after practicing some deep breathing and relaxing, mindfully observe every thought that comes by, but don't follow your thoughts around. Rather, simply observe them with interest, as a person seated in an outdoor café would observe the passersby. Your thoughts will come and go, as passersby always do, but you are the fixed element of this exercise, as you remain constantly in the present, open to the surprise.

Question of the Day: What do you think God wants, specifically, from you?

4

Scraping the Hull

The Wilderness Returns Us to Our Essence.

OUT OF WHACK

I went to the woods ... to front only the essential facts of life,
and see if I could ... learn what it had to teach, and not,
when I came to die, discover that I had not lived.
— *Henry David Thoreau (1817–1862)*

The Boundary Waters in mid-September. The aspen and maple leaves are just beginning their yellow, red, and orange glory. In another week the colors will be so brilliant that visitors will just stand in stunned silence at the display, eyes wide in disbelief. Words will fail them, and they'll tell friends back home that the photos don't do the colors justice. And they don't.

We're often taught that we need to be humble in the sight of God, and there's something to that, but right now, as I see the exuberance of the trees in front of me, and knowing the arboreal peacock that is yet to come, I wonder. Perhaps nature has it right: Offer profuse praise through the gifts we have, and just put it out there with every ounce of our sap. That's the best we can do.

These trees are not just singing; they're singing *opera*! I'm guessing it's *Carmen* or *Rigoleto*.

By this time in September, the tourists have gone, the mosquitoes are dead, the black flies have, I hope, gone to hell where they belong, and soon a group of six will be arriving from the airport in Duluth for a week of canoeing, fun, spiritual exploration, recovery, and discovery. We should have this place of almost transcendent beauty pretty much to ourselves. I'm waiting for them at the end of an upsloping dirt road that's framed by dark green, nearly black pines on either side as the sunshine makes shafts through the boughs. The weather is projected to be nearly perfect, with cool nights that are great for sleeping and warm days where the water is still swimmable. But you never know ... this is the wilderness, after all, and it's the Boundary Waters, where the weather changes quickly.

I'm especially happy to be here, and I'm looking forward with great anticipation to the week, but it's immediately clear from the body language of two of the men who get off the van that they, perhaps, are not. I always expect to see some apprehension mixed with some excitement from newcomers, but these two men seem to be carrying far more than the bags in their hands. Their faces are set like flint, their eyes glance only briefly at the scenery, with little apparent appreciation. Their noses don't seem to register the wonderful pitchy smell of the pines, and their shoulders and backs are slumped, as if carrying great weight. They look used, exhausted to the bone.

They're two ministers from the East Coast. The larger man, whom I'll call Paul, is on sabbatical; the other, whom I'll call Jerry, is here for the adventure and a chance to connect with God in a new way. In their questionnaires—something I ask participants to fill out before the trip so I'll know what their expectations are and what they're dealing with in their lives—neither had mentioned their state of exhaustion. I'm a bit concerned, but I don't have time to deal with it at the moment.

There are many things that need to get done before spending a week in the wilderness: transferring clothing from city luggage to wilderness bags—a metaphor of its own because in doing this transfer we're already learning what baggage we can leave behind and what we must absolutely take—getting the outfitter's gear; being sized for paddles and PFDs (personal flotation devices, a fancy name for life vests); and learning a bit about the gear, the place, and safety protocols. We spend some time telling our introductory stories so we'll know something about each other, then we set up our campsite, eat dinner, and clean up.

Finally, I have a chance to join Paul and Jerry at the edge of the Kawishiwi River, just as the sun is about four fingers off the horizon. The setting sun turns all the colors, including the reds, to rich and breathtaking shades of gold. There's no better time of the day for this kind of light, and it's peaceful; even the air is quiet, as if celebrating the end of a beautiful day. As the sun reclines, there's a new bite in the air, and we've all changed from shorts to pants, from T-shirts to long sleeves. On a nearby lake, a single loon yodels hopefully to other loons that do not answer back. Most of them have already headed south to the Gulf of Mexico for the winter, so our loon may be one of the last to leave.

When I arrive, Paul and Jerry are just looking, listening; they have apparently decided, finally, to savor the atmosphere, because both are chugging deep, slow draughts of the pine-fragrant air. They look a little more relaxed, and I smile, thinking ... knowing ... that the wilderness is already beginning to work its magic.

Both men are middle-aged and a bit overweight, although Jerry looks as if he may have been a wrestler when he was in school. His shoulders and back look powerfully built, and he walks with a rolling gait that says he was an athlete of sorts. Paul, the man on sabbatical, looks more stolid, with thick graying hair, a square face, and a stubble that's more white than gray. His body is taller and rounder than Jerry's. He stands about six feet to Jerry's five-foot nine, and he radiates a quiet dignity that's very reassuring. Of the two, he's the more reserved, though both men exude a certain gravitas.

They've been getting to know each other, and now that I've joined them, they begin to ask me about what we'll be doing for the week, where we'll go, what kind of food we'll eat, and so on. When the time seems right, I bring up my concern from earlier in the day:

Me: You both looked pretty tired—actually, burdened—when you got off the bus, so I want to check in with you. Are you all right? Is there something I should know?

Jerry: It's funny you'd bring that up. We were just talking about our ministries, about what they demand of us. I guess we just get used to being tired. [There's verbal agreement among the three of us, then silence for a while as we look out at the darkening river and purple sky.] One of the main reasons I'm here is to get some new perspective on my work and on my life. I try to keep my perspective, but barnacles just keep piling up. Then I lose a lot of that overview, and everything just goes out of whack. I'm feeling that way now. That's probably what you saw.

Paul: Barnacles! That's a good way of putting it, Jerry. I've never thought of it that way before, but you're right. "Barnacles" describes it perfectly.

Me: I'm from Chicago, guys, so I'm not sure what you East Coast boys mean.

Jerry: Oh. Sorry! Well, barnacles have hard shells, like clams. They live in all the oceans of the world, and there is simply no way to avoid getting them on the hull of your boat. Some paints work for a while, but the barnacles find a way ...

Me: Sort of a sailors' Field of Dreams thing: "Launch it and they will come"?

Paul: Yeah, like that. And whatever they stick to, they're there forever, even after they die. Their glue is so powerful that you can pick up a good-sized car with just a little bit of it.

Jerry: And they have barnacle friends. Lots and lots of friends, because they like to live in colonies. Once they're glued down, they can't move around to find a mate, so they build barnacle condos, one shell right on top of another, on boat hulls, on pier pilings, on rocks ... even whales.

Me: Whales, too? I had no idea ... but what's your point?

Paul: Well, the pilings and rocks aren't much of an issue, but when barnacles attach to a boat hull, if the owner doesn't do something about it within about six months, the hull gets covered with barnacles, including the rudder and propeller, and the boat weighs significantly more. Its speed and maneuverability are cut in half, and it costs about twice as much to run.

Jerry: So, the boat's just a shadow of what it's supposed to be. It's not really a boat anymore; it's a scow, a barge.

Me: So what do you do?

Paul: Well, the only thing to do is to put the boat in dry dock, then scrape, chip, or sandblast the barnacles off.

Me: And then the boat is a boat again, instead of a scow?

Jerry: Well, yes, until the barnacles start building condos again. And then the owner has to put her right again. It's a circle that just never ends.

Me: Barnacles are a great metaphor, Jerry. I'm going to use it when I make presentations ... or if I ever write a book about the wilderness and what it does for us. And, gentlemen, you have come to the right place to have your hulls scraped.

UNNEEDED BAGGAGE

Simplicity is making the journey of this life with just
baggage enough.

—*Charles Dudley Warner* (1829–1900),
American essayist and novelist

Like boats that ply oceans, in our own way we are vessels that sail
through life's waters and accumulate barnacles along the way. Our
unneeded baggage starts to weigh us down, to confuse the real purpose of living, and pretty soon we're not the joyous, bounding craft
we're meant to be.

I'm talking about things such as life-sucking busyness. Most of
us have ten pounds of things to do, but only a five-pound bag of
time.

Things such as our "keeping up with the Joneses" mentality.
The American imperative seems to be to accumulate more and
spend more, which means that we have to earn more and/or go
more deeply into debt. Which means that we work even harder.

Things such as computers, cell phones (and all the "features"
that are available for them), fax machines, personal digital assis-
tants, MP3 players, the Internet, and television.

Things such as too much work or working too much (they're
different!).

Things such as multitasking ourselves into a life that leaves
little room for us or our loved ones—and certainly no time or
space to dance with God. A life that often leads to alienation, isolation, despair, depression, perhaps even an early death.

Things such as worshipping the dogma and rituals of our religions more than we worship God.

Things such as revering the artifacts of our lives more than
the act of living itself.

Is any of this ringing a bell? Am I right in thinking this is only
a partial list?

These are just some of the barnacles we accumulate, willingly or not, thinking they're integral parts of life in the twenty-first century. So our lives speed up, almost to manic levels, but the *being* half of our "human being" slows to nearly dead in the water, and we become scows without even realizing it. We're now officially human *doings*.

Ridding ourselves of barnacles is really an act of re-simplification, of getting back to what we were meant to be: joyous, clean craft that sail freely through life's waters.

The *theory* of simplification goes back thousands of years. Twenty-five hundred years ago in Greece, Plato said, "Beauty of style and harmony and grace and good rhythm depend on simplicity." At about the same time in China, Confucius taught, "Life is really simple, but we insist on making it complicated," which was echoed by the Jewish Talmud (*Pirkei Avot* 4:1): "Who is rich? One who rejoices in one's portion"—which ultimately means, keep it simple.

In the Christian Bible Jesus told his followers:

Do not worry about your life, what you will eat, or about your body, what you will wear. For life is more than food, and the body more than clothing.... Consider the lilies, how they grow: they neither toil nor spin, yet I tell you, even Solomon in all his glory was not clothed like one of these.... And do not keep striving ... and do not keep worrying. (Luke 12:22–34)

And in the Hebrew Bible we're told:

Do not wear yourself out to get rich; be wise enough to desist. When your eyes light upon it [the next material thing], it is gone; for suddenly it takes wings to itself, flying like an eagle. (Proverbs 23:4–5)

Mahatma Gandhi, a Hindu, said, "Commonsense is the realized sense of proportion," which is an elegant way of recommending simplicity and echoes the wisdom of the preceding passage from Proverbs.

The practice of simplification also spans both time and religious boundaries. Most religions emphasize making intentional time to think about our lives and our place with God.

The Hebrew Bible psalmist puts it this way: "Be still and know that I am God" (Psalm 46:100).

In the prayer cycle of Islam, Muslims stop five times each day to give thanks and to separate briefly from the world. It's a codified practice that requires people to retreat from their busyness for a moment of reflection, to take a deep breath, gain some perspective, simplify, and go back into the world renewed and redirected.

Similarly, Jesus, in a constant ebb and flow throughout his ministry, simplified his life by leaving the people who depended on him, to be alone in the wilderness with God for prayer and renewal.

Benedictine and Buddhist monks set aside regular parts of each day to unhurriedly and rhythmically do specific tasks, not the least of which is contemplation and withdrawal so that they might slow down their internal lives and reflect on what is truly important.

The common thread of each religious practice wraps around a common theme: Don't allow the unnecessary distractions of the world to hang on to us too tightly. Or us to them.

The reality of life is, of course, that we must sail in whatever waters we find ourselves. Remaining in the harbor is safer, yes, but that is not what boats were built to do, so sail we must. The choice is whether to sail as a scow or as the smooth-sailing craft we are meant to be. But how do we rid ourselves of our barnacles?

One answer for us—and the answer of many others across many centuries—has been to go into the wilderness for some hull scraping.

THE DESERT'S QUESTION

Wilderness ... is a spiritual necessity, an antidote to the high pressure of modern life, a means of regaining serenity and equilibrium.

—*Sigurd Olson (1899–1982),*
American writer and conservationist

Why am I here, at roughly twenty degrees below zero, in the midst of this great frozen country? Why not in some place considerably more hospitable? Why not at home, where I'd be a lot more comfortable and could be thoughtfully drinking some red wine while I ponder life's big questions? Except I doubt seriously that I'd be much "available" in a civilized place. Home is home, work is work, and there's too much to do in both places, too many things asking for my attention, not to mention the kids and things to do with Jane.

No, I'm beginning to think it takes a whole new place, and a whole new set of things to do that I can't just do by rote, without thinking. Here in the wilderness, I know I have to be aware of everything I do because it's new and because if I don't, with these temperatures, the consequences could be singularly unfriendly. This total immersion, total involvement, is probably why I'm having such a remarkable time.

For the past four days I've felt more alive and more vital, more "plugged in" to everything than I've felt for years, maybe than I've ever felt. I'm in love with how all this feels because it is so simple, so straightforward, so lacking in artifice: eat, ski, keep moving, hydrate, stay warm, watch each other's backs, watch for wet spots, find a good place to camp, gather wood, cook, eat, clean up, dry our socks, feed and tether the dogs, sleep. It is, simply, what it is; nothing more, and nothing less. There are no hidden agendas out here, so unlike corporate life. The simplicity is life-restoring ... liberating.

I love discovering that I can handle the testing of the cold and the exertion and the uncertainty. I find I love the cross-country skiing. It's rhythmic, and the rhythm allows my mind to explore and ponder in ways that I don't have time for at home—and certainly not at work. It's very freeing. I am at peace in ways that are almost unknown to me, having experiences of connection to, well, creation, I guess, that are deep and true. Never in my wildest imaginings would I have expected to find such a sense of wholeness in such frozen desolation. But I'm misusing the word desolation; this place feels more pristine than bleak. The vast amounts of untracked snow and the intense silence combine to make it seem pure. The stars on clear nights are beyond counting and beyond description. And the cold is so profound it makes the place seem antiseptic because germs simply couldn't exist at these extremes. Pristine. Life is distilled to its essences.

I didn't know it when I wrote the above in my journal, but I was talking about freeing myself from the barnacles that I'd allowed to define both me and my life. I was in one of the more extreme environments in the country when I finally understood what the wilderness does for people looking for a simpler life: It puts things in proper proportion so we can recognize the difference between need and want.

In the wilderness we live with the essentials and little more, and we learn how little we truly need. What we *need* is to be safe, loved, fed, clothed, sheltered, and challenged, and above the subsistence level. Anything beyond that falls into the *want* category. With wilderness-opened eyes, we can more truly see who owns whom. Do we own our possessions, our hectic schedules, or do they own us? And does being in the wilderness eliminate our desire for things we might want but do not need? David Rensberger, author of "Deserted Places," thinks not.

Certainly the desert provides no escape from temptations and delusions. These we take with us wherever we go! But the desert, so spare and desolate, encourages and in fact requires us to strip off all that is nonessential about ourselves so that in the end we realize that, as Jesus said to Martha, "Only one thing is necessary" (Luke 10:42). "How much can you leave behind?" That is the desert's question.[1]

The first time I realized how little I needed to be profoundly happy was when I took a three-month motorcycle trip around Europe by myself. I'd never ridden a motorcycle before, so I had to learn to do that, on the English side of the road, plus basic maintenance, plus how to negotiate the different languages and currencies. I camped out everywhere I could to save money; I rode through the rain when I had to; I made good friendships with people even when we could communicate only with made-up sign language. In leaving behind all the sureties I'd ever known, I discovered a creativity, competency, and resilience in myself that astonished me and delighted me.

I had a motorcycle, a tent, a few maps, minimal camping gear, a book and my journal, some basic food, very little money, and that was it. Not much. But as I was hunkered on a riverbank just outside Meximieux, France, shaving in the cold water that had been an Alpine stream about an hour earlier, it suddenly hit me, and hard: "I'm as happy as I've ever been!" It was a life-defining moment, and in that sense it was also extremely spiritual, although I wouldn't have defined it that way at that point in my life. When I got home, explaining that minimalist happiness to my family and friends proved to be impossible. "How could you be so happy with so little?" they asked. I suspect they wouldn't have believed Thoreau either, when he said, "Most of the luxuries, and many of the so-called comforts of life, are not only not indispensable, but positive hindrances to the elevation of mankind."

But how do we know what is indispensable, what is essential? Like a person dealing with an addiction, the first step is to acknowledge what our addictions—though we may not call them that—are. We need to recognize what barnacles are weighing us down before we know what to begin scraping off. We may have unhealthy relationships that make us feel as if we "belong," but keep us from belonging to something better. We may be addicted to busyness. My primary addiction is to exercise. I can go two days, maximum, without it before I start to get disagreeable.

This isn't to say that we need to give up all the things we've come to rely on, but it is to say that we can put those things in their proper place so we can recognize the difference between need and want, and keep them in balance.

But where do we start? How do we achieve that balance?

By finding a way to retreat from daily life to learn what we don't need. By adding some challenge that is different from our normal routines, something that pushes us into unfamiliar territory (and not necessarily a *physical* territory) and makes us see things in new ways.

One study of people's wilderness experiences reported that being away from the trappings of modern civilization (and *trappings* is an appropriate word here) was key to the participants' experiences. Being in true, unsullied wilderness was exhilarating for the campers in the study, most of whom had little to no wilderness experience. The opportunity to see wildlife, to see the weather coming in and then to experience it viscerally in its full force, and to sleep under a star-filled sky were all invitations to see and to live life very differently, as the following from the author of a wilderness study shows.

> In effect, this direct contact with nature inspired many participants to identify that they very rarely "experience" the natural world in their everyday lives elsewhere, and yet in doing so, it helped them to "get in touch" ... with more important spiritual matters.[2]

Those who say the wilderness is empty miss the point entirely: It is, in fact, overflowing with possibility. We simply have to see "emptiness" differently. When we're able to separate from the things that keep us so busy, we can stop the clatter in our minds, and the mental and spiritual dust begins to settle. Then we can look with clarity at the whole complex ball of our lives.

That said—and I think it's completely true—I need to add two important clarifications. First, we don't have to go to extremes to find such places. A *taste* of the wilderness, and the freedom it offers, is available any time we can distance our-selves from life-sucking "things" to create room for things of greater importance. (But please notice that I use the word *taste* to qualify a non-wilderness experience, for while it can be pow-erful it is just a hint of what's available in true wilderness.) Go to a park or a garden with some intentionality and a willingness to see the Divine in small things, a willingness to be surprised and changed, and you might be amazed at how much even a small amount of direct contact with nature changes your perspective.

Second, although the wilderness can help us see our addic-tions, the barnacles we carry, it cannot scrape us clean of our desire for them. It just shows us what they are and what they are not, what life is like without them, and perhaps the ways we can deal with them.

One definition of *nature* is "the intrinsic or essential character of somebody or something." That works very nicely for this discus-sion. The natural world is what it is, without any makeup, and it is exactly what it needs to be. And exposure to it affects us the same way. When we are in it, it helps us know exactly what we are, without makeup—our intrinsic and essential character—and exactly what we need to be. For those who seek authenticity in their lives, this is an immeasurable gift.

FRESH VISION

Nature often holds up a mirror so we can see more clearly
the ongoing processes of growth, renewal, and transformation in our lives.

—*Frederic and Mary Ann Brussat,*
Spiritual Literacy

For at least forty-one centuries, human beings in all parts of the
world have retreated to wild places, far from the din of civilization,
to get re-centered. The noise of communal living and the compe-
tition that always persists there drown out the peace and perspective that come when people can live—even temporarily—in quiet
and natural places, a sentiment echoed by Elizabeth Canham,
author of *A Table of Delight: Feasting with God in the Wilderness*:

> In the desert, a place of holy encounter, we hear God's call.
> The Hebrew and Christian scriptures make it clear that
> spiritual formation often takes place in the desert, where
> stark emptiness strips us of pretense and silence wraps itself
> around us. In the desert ... motivations are revealed; we
> relinquish baggage [i.e., barnacles]; we receive fresh vision.[3]

Take, for example, the biblical story of the forty years of desert trial
and wandering of the people of Israel; it occupies more than 20
percent of the Hebrew Bible. I know of no longer example that
involves more people (six hundred thousand) than this wilderness
experience of hull scraping. It is perhaps the most perfect example
of an entire people whose identity was smelted, then reforged, in
the desert and mountain wildernesses.

For four hundred years prior to their release, the Israelites had
been enslaved by the Egyptians, as God had told Abraham they
would be for neglecting the covenant God had made with them.
Their long history of slavery—roughly ten generations—bred a
slave mentality from their soles to their scalps, with all the emo-

tional, mental, psychological, physical, and spiritual barnacles that must have weighed those people down.

God's plan was to take this ragtag mob through the Sinai Desert to the land of Canaan, "a land flowing with milk and honey" (Exodus 3:17). But why *that* route? If you look at a map of the Middle East of four thousand years ago, you will see very quickly that there was an easier way. Why go the long way around?

Rabbis argue that God took the Israelites through the difficulties of the Sinai precisely *because* the desert route was more difficult, that God used the harshness and sparseness of the desert to show the Hebrews their utter dependence on God, and to make them hard enough to govern themselves. As Jungian analyst Edward Edinger observed, "Man's extremity is God's opportunity,"[4] and God was going to make use of human extremity to teach some important lessons and recast a people.

But a few weeks of desert trial were not enough to reconfigure a tribe accustomed to many generations of slavery. In spite of all the ways God guided and supported the Israelites—a pillar of fire by night and a pillar of dust during the day to guide and comfort them; quail and manna falling from the sky to feed them; water flowing from a rock to quench their thirst—the people were not prepared to accept some risk and endure some hardship to learn how to become masters (with God's help) of their own destiny. They preferred the sure bread of slavery and the total certainty of their misery to the uncertainty of a new future:

> If only we had died by the hand of the Lord in the land of Egypt, when we sat by the fleshpots and ate our fill of bread; for you have brought us out into this wilderness to kill this whole assembly with hunger. (Exodus 16:3)

> Why did you bring us out of Egypt, to kill us and our children and livestock with thirst? (Exodus 17:4)

God realized that these people were not ready to become a nation, so it took forty years of wandering, in a desert they could have crossed in a matter of weeks, for the wilderness to scrape the hull of the entire tribe of the bonds of slavery and forge them into a stronger, more self-determining people. Their entire identity was re-formed by the hardships they faced in the desert.

The wilderness was of such bedrock importance to the Israelites' growth as a people that 70 percent of the first five books of the is set in the wilderness. The Hebrew word for the book Numbers (*Bemidbar*) is more correctly translated as "In the Wilderness." In that book, the "desert is purgative and revelatory, and it provides the single most formative experience in the creation of the Jewish people and of Christians as well."[5] It is so formative to their history that any other hardship they face is compared to their time in the desert.

Critical to our understanding of how we can find renewal in our own lives is the recognition that the renewal of Israel's covenant with God could happen only in the vulnerability of that desert experience. Because their need for complete security—even the "security" of slavery—was too great, nothing transformative could happen with God because they didn't trust either God or themselves enough to be vulnerable. Only in a land where they were far past easy and deep into risky could the real learning take place. Only with the gift of hindsight could they realize that it was *because* of their trial in the wilderness that they could finally claim their identity as the chosen people of God.

> As I reflect back on the trip, I wouldn't have changed anything because the challenges of what we were doing leading up to the solo made the trip what it was. Had I not had the challenges, I would not have begun to think about the boundaries that define me and define my life and the way I think and the way I approach things. I would have come for solitude, but I would have come with my old mind-set. Each of the experiences went

beyond anything I could have done on my own.... The combination of the spiritual, physical, mental, and emotional really forced me to look at things in an entirely different way.... It was life altering for me.

—Susan Turner, on a canoe trip
in the Boundary Waters Canoe Area

In our culture of comfort and avoidance of the hard things that require us to be blindingly candid about our lives, I know I'm asking a lot when I say we need to put ourselves in the path of a wilderness challenge. But we do carry many things that weigh us down and confuse the essence of *who* we are—the beauty of *what* we are—and this baggage does not go away without some serious and intent examination. This is the gift of the wilderness. It is God's "hull scraper," stripping us of the barnacles of civilization that slow us, distract us, and divert us in our pursuit of God—and God's pursuit of us.

QUESTIONS FOR REFLECTION

- What feels "out of whack" in your life right now? What "barnacles" are weighing you down?

- What are your addictions? If you're tempted to say, "I don't have any," expand your definition of addiction. Include nonmaterial things, such as an addiction to being busy, and so forth. Make an honest list; you may be surprised.

- Ask yourself the "desert question": How much can I leave behind? Make a two-column list with your *needs* on the left and your *wants* on the right. Prayerfully consider the balance.

- What would you like to do to simplify your life? How would you go about it?

- Where could you go this week to give yourself some direct contact with nature? Plan a time and place where you can create some mental distance from "life-sucking" things. While you're there, breathe deeply and keep your mind and heart open to what your "wilderness"—no matter its size or location—has to teach you.

NOTES

5

GOD IN A BOX
THE WILDERNESS TAKES US BEYOND OUR EXPECTATIONS INTO GOD'S SURPRISES.

HANDCUFFED TO EXPECTATIONS

God is not what you imagine or what you think you understand.

—*St. Augustine (354–430 CE)*

In the pre-trip questionnaires people fill out before starting a Renewal in the Wilderness trip, one of the key questions, from a spiritual standpoint, asks, "What are your expectations of how you might experience God?"

Sometimes the answer is "I don't know what to expect," but after years of leading people into the wilderness and watching their expectations unfold, I've learned that "I don't know" is usually a top-of-mind answer. When they dig a bit deeper, they find many expectations, and those expectations are often the Killers of Possibility. In the same way that gravity can bend light, expectations—whether spoken or not—can bend, or even block completely, a person's experience of divine presence.

Mental health professionals tell us—as if we needed confirmation—that humans break down psychologically when confronted with too much chaos, which is why we try so hard to build predictability and control into our lives, even if it's illusory. If we believe that this concept also applies to our spiritual lives, then we do everything we can to diminish God's creative unpredictability by reverse engineering God in our image, forgetting that it is the other way around.

Many of our unexamined expectations *of* God—and prejudices *about* God—come from childhood, from Sunday school or other religious training. The biblical stories many of us were taught have built expectations in our minds about how we imagine God will be revealed, primarily in hugely dramatic and memorable ways: pillars of fire, columns of dust, a burning bush, a voice in the clouds, parting waters or walking on them, healing the lame, raising the dead, and so on.

Problems—and often cynicism—erupt, however, when our expectations and our experience collide. And if our spiritual expectations are based on someone else's standards—especially if they're impossible burning-bush standards—they ultimately betray us.

Twenty-six hundred years ago, the Buddha shared his wisdom about accepting the expectations of others in the Third Noble Truth:

> Do not believe in anything simply because you have heard it. Do not believe in anything simply because it is spoken and rumored by many. Do not believe in anything simply because it is found written in your religious books. Do not believe in anything merely on the authority of your teachers and elders. Do not believe in traditions because they have been handed down for many generations. But after observation and analysis [and, I would add, the experience of your heart], when you find that anything agrees with reason and is conducive to the good and benefit of one and all, then accept it and live up to it.

The *Masnavi*, a collection of mystical Sufi works attributed to Rumi that is second only to the Qur'an in importance in the Muslim faith, makes a similar assertion in the second story of book 4:

> Would he had been less full of borrowed knowledge! Then he would have accepted inspired knowledge.... Traditional knowledge, when inspiration is available, is like making ablutions in sand when water is near. Make yourself ignorant, be submissive, and then you will obtain release from your ignorance.

In the Christian New Testament, Jesus taught people to discard all expectations of how he should behave. For example, he forgave sinners, which upset the establishment hierarchy because only God could do such things! He forgave a woman whose "sins were many" because she repented fully and authentically, and offered him more hospitality than his host (Luke 7:36–50). Then there is the story of Jesus meeting the Samaritan woman at the well. Not only did Jews hate the Samaritans in those days, but for a rabbi to speak to a strange woman of any nationality was unheard of and scandalous. When Jesus's disciples found him, "they were astonished that he was speaking with a woman" (John 4:1–42).

Throughout the four New Testament gospels of Matthew, Mark, Luke, and John, Jesus did the unexpected, defying society's code of behavior in this tightly wrapped, tradition-bound tribal culture. He broke the rule that prohibited work—even healing—on the Sabbath. He mingled with the unclean (a violation of protocol in itself) and healed a leper. He even healed non-Jews. His actions paint a picture of a man far less concerned with what humans thought was right than with what God told him was right.

So, if we need historical precedent and theological weight behind us to begin dealing with our expectations, then we have it from many sources. In one form or another, all these spiritual leaders are asking us to abandon expectations of how things should be.

They're asking us not to put a box around God in an effort to contain, predict, or control God.

On the first day of each Renewal in the Wilderness trip, I thank people for telling me what their expectations are. I talk about the issue of expectations, of how we put God in the box of "how God must appear so that we recognize the appearance." I suggest that when we attempt to put God in this kind of box, we create a stronger relationship with our expectations than we do with God. In whatever way we attempt to contain God, it certainly cannot keep God in, but it is very effective at keeping *us* out. Who among us, operating with expectations of seeing God only in biblical proportions, would suddenly understand that we're seeing the magnificence of God in a hummingbird?

Yet most of us are resistant to examining our expectations because they help us (we think) establish some predictability in our messy world. Part—maybe a large part—of our identity is handcuffed to our expectations, and personal identity is not something we relinquish or change easily.

Some realistic expectations are good, of course, such as how we'll conduct ourselves, what level of competence we'll expect from ourselves, and so forth. But the bottom line is that, in spiritual pursuits, if we're too needy of control, if we're too addicted to our expectations, very little can happen with God.

"LET GO AND LET GOD"

> In wilderness people can find ... an experience of the eternal mystery ... a sense of the sacredness of all creation.
> —*Sigurd Olson (1899–1982),*
> *American writer and conservationist*

After our group members talk about what expectations they bring—for the physical aspects of our trip, for hopes of a spiritual experience, for hopes to reconnect with nature or God or people—I ask them to leave their expectations behind, as much as they are able, so that they'll be open to the unexpected moments of gift.

I talk about my cumulative observations from many wilderness trips, and my personal experience, that when we let God be God—that is, the God who created us, rather than the God we create—startling and transcendent things happen. "Let go and let God," the mantra of twelve-step programs, applies equally to those of us who are addicted to our expectations. When we get out of God's way and open our hearts—and maybe even our minds—to the ways God will choose to be revealed, life views and God views are rejiggered.

For most people, this change happens at a gut level; it is not an intellectual thing at all.

> One of the reasons I went on the trip was to examine a question I had been struggling with about God, particularly what does it mean that God is omnipotent when there is so much disaster, hate, and war in the world. We did not have time to discuss that question, or other questions I had in mind. For this reason one may wonder how much of a religious experience this was.
>
> However, the religious experience was not the anticipated discussion of God, but rather feeling God work through us. Although we started to discuss the questions presented to the group, the conversation soon moved to listening to a woman who was recently widowed talk about her grief and the problems she was having adjusting to the loss of her husband. Others talked about themselves and their life experience. We listened to each other with compassion. We were all reassured by the group. This, ultimately, was more rewarding than searching for answers to unanswerable questions about God.
>
> Five strangers had worked together, lived in the present, given up our expectations, and had the challenges of the river

and the camping. We had perhaps experienced God working
through us by caring for each other, and in caring for each other
we also cared for ourselves. I experienced the wilderness as a
sacred place.

—William R. Wallin, on a canoe trip
on the Wisconsin River

By broadening his spiritual horizon, William was able to get beyond his expectation of how God "should" work to see, instead, how God does work through acts of human compassion.

In a different wilderness, a man participated in a vision quest and, like William, came loaded with expectations. On a vision quest the supplicant is left alone in the wilderness, exposed to the forces of nature for three or four days. During that time, the supplicant fasts, hoping God's spirit will visit in some form—in something as large as a thunderstorm or as small as an ant. The supplicant's sole mission is to be in a hopeful attitude of openness to whatever comes.

As this man described his experience, however, he found all his expectations frustrated until he could release those expectations and give himself over to whatever happened:

I waited for the big moment of enlightenment. Nothing happened. Nothing at all, not even the slightest miracle.

Two days were filled with absolutely nothing but silence. Since I had one day left, I decided to spend my remaining time simply enjoying myself. At the time it really didn't feel like a choice.

There and then my life changed!

In that moment, in my circle of stones, my lifelong belief system of needing to struggle and make an effort to achieve success changed. I felt a deep sense of peace fill me. Those days in the beauty of the silence brought me to the decision to ... use my time for growth and adventure.[1]

There is a wonderful Sufi parable about a stream trying to make its way across a desert. It had managed to conquer all the mountain and valley obstacles right up to the edge of the desert, and it expected to conquer the sand as well. But the stream quickly found that the sand absorbed all its moisture and blocked its progress. When the desert told the stream to turn into vapor so it could be carried across the desert on the wind, the stream protested. After all, if it gave itself up to the wind, what reassurance was there that it would still be a stream? So it kept trying to move forward across the desert in the same way it had before.

But the stream failed and failed and failed again, constantly pouring its precious life-water into the same place in the desert. It could make no progress across the sponge of sand.

"Why can't I remain the same stream that I am?" the stream cried out in frustration.

The desert answered, ever so wisely: "You never can remain what you are. Either you become a swamp or you give yourself to the winds."[2]

Sometimes we must give ourselves to the metaphorical wind—or, as I've found on some canoe trips, the not-so-metaphorical wind! As the desert counseled, we must, sometimes—perhaps many times—relinquish our expectations of the way things should be and open ourselves to the winds that will take us to an improved, but furiously unknown, future. Not an easy thing.

Sometimes it is necessary to go as deeply as possible into nature, away from as much civilized interference as possible, to leave our expectations behind and be open to wherever, however, the wind might carry us and reform us.

This dynamic was played out on an October canoe trip on the Wisconsin River. Susan, one of the participants, was a very talented woman who had achieved substantial material and social success, and she was used to—perhaps addicted to—constant stimulation, the juggling act of doing fifteen things at once, and, as a consummate marketer, the art of the deal. Her track was fast and her success "fed" her, but life had recently dealt her a serious body blow, and she recognized that her journey to the wilderness was a chance to slow down, take stock, and get back in touch with herself and with things that carry more meaning.

The part of the Wisconsin River where we canoed is a beautiful, uninhabited part of the river. Surprisingly, we did not see the furry animals I expected. Birds, yes, but no deer or raccoons or muskrat, although we saw their footprints whenever we stopped.

I was struck by the fact that the scenery was beautiful and serene but monotonous. One beautiful hill gave way to another beautiful hill; one lovely island was succeeded by another, and the fiery red maples were replaced by shimmering yellow river birch. In the midst of all this beauty and serenity, I found myself waiting for something more exciting ... something more dramatic to take place. I kept hoping to see another bald eagle around the next bend in the river, perhaps swooping down from the sky to grab a fish from the river, right in front of us, and then disappear over the tree line. But it didn't come. I was aware of waiting for "something more" to happen. I could almost hear my inner director say, "Cue the eagle."

About halfway through the trip, I realized how often I have the same expectations in my everyday life. Rather than being content and present to the steady, ongoing, non-scenic moments of my day, I keep waiting for something more exciting to occur. And in the process of living breathlessly waiting, I miss the lovely subtle, simple changes and textures of the day.

I know that my expectations also kill most of the spontaneity that could be a rich part of my life, but I've ignored those moments because they haven't conformed to how I expected they should look, or what I expected they should be.

I have learned a lot on this trip. Being put in demanding, potentially uncomfortable, and unpredictable situations challenges my expectations and calls up my most free and flexible self!

—Susan B. Larson, on a canoe trip
on the Wisconsin River

Susan, who had created very high expectations for herself, was learning to pull herself away from the box, to welcome unexpected moments of grace.

Another seeker, Ed, stumbled into a similar moment of unexpected grace on a hike in the Wasatch Mountains of Utah, outside Park City:

The mountains around me absorb my words. It is quiet except for the wind in the fan-shaped leaves of the aspens and the whisper of small streams. The trail leads finally to a small lake in a clearing, and a younger man is there, sunning himself on the bank with a mountain bike beside him.

As I pass him, he says hello. He is the first person I have talked to on the trails in three days. We talk for an hour, and Pete [not his real name] tells me his story of recovery from alcoholism, six years of sobriety … how he's found himself in some pretty honest days working the steps of AA. I share my story of what brought me to these mountains, and of my own younger days, and of my working in a prison in East St. Louis.

As men can and will do in these unexpected moments, we share deeper stories about past loves, about losses, about recovery. As I prepare my pack to head south to Big Cottonwood, Pete stops for a moment and gives me a hug. "Hey man, I've appreciated our talk. I've learned a lot from you. Thanks for the exchange of words."

I give him my last "older man/mentor" thoughts: "If we pay attention to harvesting the good in ourselves, then that is what we will find; if we look for the bad, that will be there, too."

Pete's eyes are wet, and mine are, too. He says, "I'm try-
ing to learn that; it's a hard lesson to learn, but I'm getting
there."

We part.

I head slowly down the path to the road and pick wildflow-
ers all the way.

—Edward Ravine

Faced with some major decisions, Ed had come to the mountains
to wrestle with his life: "I had expected to listen to the voice inside
me. I discovered, instead, the voice of faith. In the silence in my
heart (and the heart of the mountains) I could hear God speak."
Through the wilderness experience, Ed and Pete were freed to see
the grace of small brushes with the Divine in ways neither man
expected.

Releasing our expectations allows us to walk in this world
with fewer blinders. "People see God every day," Pearl Bailey once
said, "they just don't recognize him." In order to "see God," we
need to get past the walls we've created to contain God—but
which in reality keep us out. Only then can we notice the open
door to God's surprise.

THE DOOR TO SURPRISE

As you sit on the hillside, or lie prone under the trees of
the forest, or sprawl wet-legged by a mountain stream,
the great door, that does not look like a door, opens.
—*Stephen Graham,* The Gentle Art of Tramping

The Incas walked these trails, once. Their fabled culture and jaw-
dropping works are all around us in the ruins we encounter as we
hike deeper and higher into the Peruvian Andes. One of the
Quechua natives (who are descendants of the Inca) we meet,
Amaru, says reverentially, "These are *sahkrid* [sacred] mountains,

you know. The gods live here, and the Inca himself [the king of the civilization that was named for him] came to these very mountains to worship. A very ... *sahkrid* ... place!" He pauses between the words for emphasis.

We can feel the sacredness. The Andes are mythically high and rugged; they're 100 percent can't-believe-my-eyes beautiful. But what makes them different from any mountains I've ever seen is that they're so closely spaced. It's as if, at Creation, God was playing at the beach, making sand-dribble cones one right next to the other. Lots of them, and *very* tall. Because they're so close to each other, and so lushly green—up to almost fourteen thousand feet (by comparison, vegetation stops in the Rockies at about eight thousand feet)—they are the most "personal" mountains I've ever been in. They feel almost friendly because they seem to beckon us in. But that impulse is quickly tempered by the rolls of fog that appear, then disappear, on the trail, on the horizon, and over the ruins. It is a mystical place, with the inviting pull of divine relationship balanced equally with the push of divine mystery. For my eyes, the yin and yang of this whole setting—the invitation tempered by the push—is a metaphor for the relationship with God.

On the second day of our trek, the group chooses to bypass the ruins of Sayac Marca, but I am strongly drawn there. Perhaps it's because a narrow, precipitous trail leads to the ruins, making it genuinely remote; perhaps I hope to have a remarkable view at the promontory; perhaps it's because there is mystery waiting there that sings a quiet song of allure. Perhaps it's all of those, so I head off by myself.

The fog is too thick for the view I'd hoped to find, but because there are no views to distract my eyes, I focus entirely on what the Incas built seven hundred years ago. I am agog once more at their engineering genius, crafting masterpiece structures out of stone and little else. Room leads to room leads to passageway leads to protective outer walls, and at the end of the ruins, in a round room with a window that looks out on the fog-enshrouded valley, I stop. These circular areas are holy places; this is a *sahkrid* room.

I sit on a finished stone in the middle of the floor to imagine what it must have been like in this world, in this place, nearly eighteen generations ago. Except for the low wind and occasional bird calls, it is completely silent.

In that holy roofless room, alone with my thoughts, I experience an unbidden and overwhelming sense of wholeness, a feeling that the world is exactly right, and I am absorbed into it as an integral part. I feel peace in my whole being, for about two minutes, and then it slowly wanes.

This moment of grace takes me by surprise because it is completely unexpected; I had no spiritual expectations of this trip. I had come to the Andes purely for the adventure, not for such an intimate encounter with God. But, once again, God defied my expectations, as if saying: "Do not expect me to do the expected. Do not attempt to box me in with your need to control me. Do not try to predict me." As God said to Isaiah, "I am about to do a new thing":

> A voice cries out: "In the wilderness prepare the way of the Lord, make straight in the desert a highway for our God. Every valley shall be lifted up, and every mountain and hill be made low; the uneven ground shall become level, and the rough places a plain. Then the glory of the Lord shall be revealed.... Do not remember the former things, or consider the things of old. *I am about to do a new thing;* now it springs forth, do you not perceive it? I will make a way in the wilderness and rivers in the desert." (Isaiah 40:3–5, 43:18–9) [italics added]

Despite our best efforts to contain God and make God predictable, God will not live *down* to our expectations. And, as Isaiah suggests, God is revealed in "the wilderness and rivers," in places beyond the tentacles of civilization. More than almost any other place, the wilderness lays us open to the surprise of God. Thoreau understood this perfectly when he declared that we need the stimulant of wild places that can carry us "beyond [ourselves], beyond all illusion of mastery, into an emptiness that [leaves us] stunned, vulnerable, and open to the unexpected."

Without question, God's presence and handiwork are found in the big wilderness settings, whether lush or arid, mountains or desert, summer or winter. But I have to emphasize, especially for the couch potatoes among us, that manifestations of God in very ordinary places are available almost daily—not just in the wilderness—*if* we're available to be surprised. *If* we're not wedded to our expectations. And when we recognize them as daily possibilities, God no longer seems distant or absent.

The eleventh-century Jewish Spanish poet Judah Halevi balanced the divine-in-the-ordinary dichotomy perfectly in his question, "Lord, where shall I find You?" followed by the equally haunting, yin vs. yang, question, "And where shall I not find You?"[3] These ancient questions sound remarkably similar to Frank's questions about his encounter with the hummingbird.

I sat on that stone in that sacred round room in the Incan ruins for about fifteen more minutes, long after the moment of grace had passed. But it hadn't really passed, of course. As I walked out of the holy room and back out to the trail, I remembered Emerson's lines: "Standing on the bare ground—my head bathed by the blithe air and uplifted into infinite space ... the currents of the Universal Being circulate through me; I am part or particle of God."[4]

Nothing could have explained my moment better. Nothing is more evocative of what happens to us when we release our expectations and remember to watch for the "door that does not look like a door."

QUESTIONS FOR REFLECTION

Whatever your understanding of God is, it sets up expectations of how you think God can be experienced, so it is important to recognize what you expect.

- What is your concept of who or what God is, and of what God's role is? A loving parent? A finger-wagging, judgmental, and punishing deity? Something in between?

- As you examine your spiritual expectations, ask yourself *whose* expectations they really are. Do they come from childhood, from something you were taught, or do they come from your own experience?

- How well do your *expectations* of God match your *experience* of God?

- How well are your spiritual expectations serving you? How much room do they allow you for growth and change? Are there any expectations you would like to let go of or see differently?

- Have you ever had a startling experience of God—even if you didn't define it as "God" at the time—in a natural setting? What struck you—and stuck with you—the most about the experience?

- Each day this week, keep a lookout for God's surprises, for the "door that does not look like a door." If you keep a journal, write down the small things that occur each day that might be a brush with God in the middle of the ordinary. Periodically review your journal to see what graces have brushed you.

NOTES

6

GOD ON THE EDGE
THE WILDERNESS TAKES US BEYOND OUR COMFORT ZONE, TESTS US, AND TEACHES US.

LEAVING PREDICTABLE

Often the difference between a full life and a cramped existence is measured in terms of our opportunities to test our physical strength against the elements of the wilderness.

—*W. K. Merrill,*
The Hiker's & Backpacker's Handbook

In the beautiful hills of western North Carolina, just outside of Brevard, are some of the most challenging mountain biking trails in the country. The mountains here in the Pisgah Forest aren't like the Rockies. They're much older, very worn down and rounded, and much more sensual than they are imposing. They're probably not more than six thousand feet high, but for mountain biking, they are lung-burning, heart-pumping, and leg-trashing nonetheless. We're here for a lot of fun, but we're also here to test ourselves, to "push our envelopes," to see what our potential is outside our comfort zones.

Unlike some mountains in the West, these are in the middle of a rain forest. As in the Amazon and the other mostly equatorial rain forests of the world, it rains sixty to seventy-five inches a year here, so the trails are perpetually soft. The soil is so absorbent of the rain, you can almost hear the ground swallow. The ground next to the trails is even softer, so at least we usually land on gentle earth when we fall off our bikes.

And I fall off my bike five times before lunch on the first day.

This just doesn't happen! I'm amazed and embarrassed—I've ridden far too much to fall like this, and it bruises my ego. I take scant comfort in the fact that everyone else is falling, too. The trails and roots and rocks we ride over are slick with moisture, so the knobby tires slide out from under us, and we fall. Sections of the trails are sometimes so soft that the tires won't bite well, or they just sink into the loam, and we fall. By lunchtime, our curses have stopped, mostly, and have been replaced with laughter as we adjust our egos, wipe off the mud, and go on.

When we stop to rest, we take time to look around at the rain-plumped beauty of the Pisgah Forest. It is a magical place, with trees so big around and mossy, and undergrowth so dense and resplendent with many shades of green, that it boggles our collective minds. Who knew green came in so many colors? In many places we can look into the ancient growth of the hills and see enormous trees that have crashed into other trees at crazy angles. Sunshine filters through the leaves in humidity-shafted pokes of light that sketchily illuminate the forest floor and the ferns that grow everywhere in immense profusion. It smells rich and fertile and moist, and it strikes us as a place so primal that we wouldn't be totally surprised to see dinosaurs grazing in the distance.

Then we're off again, pounding down and up the trails, learning how to read the ground better so we don't fall so often, and we're having a fine, fine time. This is as good as it gets, we think, and we consciously *don't* think about the trees that line the side of the trail as we descend, often at twenty miles an hour. A blown tire or a moment's inattention, or a front tire grazing a stone or log the wrong way, could easily send us flying off the trail and into those trees. There are consequences for errors of these kinds, but we choose to shove acknowledgment of them to the part of our brains—the teenager part—that tells us we're bulletproof and immortal. The endorphins are pumping through us wildly, like a snowmelt-fed creek, and our sense of well-being and utter happiness is sometimes just overpowering. It is joyous to be here and to be alive! Ah, wilderness!

Each night we camp in a different place, beside mountain streams, beneath the behemoth trees, and under the wavering, humidity-refracted stars. We are so far from civilization that on overcast nights our eyes cannot adjust to the obsidian blackness. We never hear owls at night, and we speculate that the Pisgah Forest is just too dark, even for them.

To haul our week of supplies, we each pull aluminum, one-wheeled trailers that hold about fifty pounds. They're called Beasts of Burden, or BOBs for short, and pulling them fully loaded changes the dynamics and freedom of riding a bike. Going downhill, with fifty pounds of gear in the trailer pushing us faster than we want to go, the BOB's wheel sometimes breaks loose when we don't brake properly, and the BOB slides around the rider, off the trail, pulling us with it. It makes things interesting, but no one's been hurt—we just quickly learn not to follow each other too closely.

The BOBs work well as long as we choose our trails carefully to avoid steep inclines and impossibly tight switchbacks. We stick mostly to dirt access roads because they're more predictable and not so steep, but to get to our campsites, we have to abandon the roads for the trails, often for a mile or two. We swap predictable for narrow, rocky, and dicey.

This is a wonderful metaphor for spiritual renewal—and for life renewal as well: leaving the known, the safe and predictable, and going to deeper, wilder places in ourselves, closer to the edge, where it can be narrow, rocky, and dicey. Without this kind of challenge, without this kind of edginess, not much happens. On some level, we know this, either *because* we've been tested—or because we have *not*, as this sojourner on a solitary desert retreat reflected:

> *The severity of the desert inspired many of the world's religions.*
> *The stripping away of things we most desire—sex, entertainment, acquisition, political power—shows us it is God alone who can satisfy our deepest want....*
>
> *My own sojourn into the desert includes a comfortable bed, a (gas) heated room, and simple, exquisite meals.... I'm not hungry, hot or cold, thirsty, lonely, or on the edge in any way that will push my boundaries—and perhaps just so, I'm not likely to ... be granted a glimpse of the Divine.*
>
> —Jason Byassee, on a visit to a desert monastery

It's been my experience—and an experience well documented in most established religions—that God is not the God of comfortable places. God usually doesn't visit us in life-changing ways at our desks or in our easy chairs. Spiritually or otherwise, places on the edge—wilderness places (of any kind)—have much to teach us. It's always been this way.

In the Bible the wilderness was consistently a place of testing and of revelation. When Pharaoh asked Moses where he was taking the Israelite slaves, Moses replied, as God's spokesman: "Let my people go, so that they may celebrate a festival to me in the wilderness" (Exodus 5:1). The Israelites left all the trappings and "safety" of civilization to go to a marginal place as a marginal people, where they would be refined and rebuilt into a people that could rule a nation.

In the third, fourth, and fifth centuries, the Desert Fathers and Mothers left their urban areas to carve out a space in the Sahara Desert where they could come face-to-face with themselves, in all their frailty, and with God, in all God's strength and mercy. To find what was at their center, they went to the edges of both the landscape and their own physical needs.

Among the American Plains Indians, the tradition of the vision quest required young boys at puberty (sometimes girls, depending on the tribe) to get away from the distractions of society and go to the edge to be alone with the Great Spirit. They would spend about four days alone in the wilderness (usually in a high place), in prayer and fasting, exposed to all the forces of nature in the hopes of having a vision of what the Great Spirit (*Wakan-Tanka*) wanted from them as adults, and how the personal manifestation of *Wakan-Tanka* would help in their quest.

The Great Spirit could come to them in any form—earthworm or lightning bolt—so the supplicants had to be keenly attuned to whatever animals, natural things, or visions came to them. The candidates had to prove their worthiness, so ritual suffering, prayer, true humility, and privation helped them make their case to the Divine. It was believed that the messenger of *Wakan-Tanka*, who would be their guardian for life, awoke the voice of God that was already in the supplicant.[1]

The common thread among these wilderness experiences and religious traditions is that, to have a life-changing experience of God, we need to be in a place where we can be open to God's courtship. We need to be in a place that reminds us of who God is, and who we are.

CONFRONTING OUR LIMITS

> When written in Chinese, the word crisis is composed of two characters. One represents danger, and the other represents opportunity.
>
> —*John F. Kennedy (1917–1963)*

On the first day of our mountain biking trip, I do a quick orientation ride to discover the quirks of my bike. At a remote corner of the outfitter's property, I come across one of those high ropes courses, but this one is different from any I've seen. This course is on the side of a steep hill that has been cleared of timber, and there are three impossibly tall, straight poles set into the side of the slope in a triangular fashion, with one pole at the bottom of the slope, and the other two poles, equally spaced, about twenty-five yards up the hill. I can't tell how tall the poles actually are because the tops are lost in a dense fog, but as I look at the gyre of thin wires that snake up and up the triangle in successively higher levels, each level looks more difficult, more Machiavellian, than the preceding level.

My whole body gives an intense, involuntary shudder, and I thank God that I don't have to do this ropes course! I'm almost pathologically afraid of heights, so I am very grateful the ropes course is not a part of this bike trip.

Ten minutes later, back at the outfitter's base camp, my safe world is knocked off center: The outfitter offers us the "chance" to do the ropes course when we come back, at the end of our biking. "It's a great way to cap off a wonderful mountain adventure," he says. The rest of the group is enthusiastic. I offer a sincere prayer for lightning and high winds—the only reasons he wouldn't let us climb.

The week just blazes by, and far too quickly. I eat well, I sleep, not thinking much about the future, not thinking much about the ropes course. But on the final morning as we pack our BOBs for the last time, I begin to give some thought to the ropes course—positive, this time.

What a great opportunity to confront my phobia. "When I get back home," I tell myself, "I can ride glass-enclosed elevators without having to face the back and close my eyes."

"If," I think confidently, "I can rocket down these trails in utter disregard for mortality, then what have I to fear from a little stationary ropes course? I'll even have a safety harness, which I certainly don't have on the bike." So I'm calm. Mature.

We clean up the gear, turn it in, then check out the harnesses and helmets we'll need for the afternoon. We have a light lunch, then walk over to the ropes course. The endorphins from the morning are still greasing my confidence.

When we reach the course, the fog that had obscured the tops of the poles a week earlier is gone, and my calm centeredness does a stutter step. The poles are higher than I thought possible, and the wires are nearly invisible from the ground. I can hear the wind humming and whistling through the wires.

"My God ... ohmyGod, what have I gotten myself into?" A familiar fear creeps back into my gut, and my confidence begins bleeding, like a slow leak in a balloon.

The instructors arrive and show us how to get into the harnesses and secure them so they won't slip, how to use our carabiners (aluminum safety devices used to fasten climbing ropes to belaying equipment) to clip onto the safety wires above us, and how to transfer the carabiner from one wire to the next without falling. They give us pointers about moving from one level to the next and tell us how the teamwork challenge operates at the top level.

About eighty feet from the ground—the teamwork challenge level—there are two horizontal wires, mostly parallel to each other, about four feet apart. Starting from a small platform about the size of two baseball bases, two people face each other and walk sideways along the wires holding each other's shoulders, leaning weight against weight, and coordinating their shuffling side steps to be in sync. The wires are tight but not steady, so that slight swing must be coordinated as well. As the partners progress down the wires, the wires get farther apart, and the partners lean more into each other, arching more and more over the void. It is a truly diabolical system, and it requires a lot of trust in your partner, and a lot of communication.

"At the end of the course," the instructors continue blithely, "the only way off the ropes tower is in the 'Chair of Death.' You'll love it!" And then they ask for volunteers.

My breathing has become shallow and rapid, my pulse has no spaces, my palms are sweaty, and I've developed an anvil headache. The endorphins have been replaced by "fight or flight" adrenaline, and my fine oratory about being able to look out from glass elevators turns to flaccid bravado.

One of my recurring childhood nightmares was to be at the top of a tall, flexible pole that swayed slowly back and forth, gathering speed and arc with each swing, until finally ... well, I'd always wake up before "finally," so I don't know for sure. And here I am, about to live my nightmare. I am, without mincing words, scared almost to death. My whole body is tingling from unconscious hyperventilation. I had wanted to be pushed to the edge, but I didn't really mean—I certainly never intended—to the edge of a real abyss!

I volunteer to go second, knowing that if I have to wait, I'll never do it. Then I begin pacing madly just to burn off some anxiety, and I start to babble-pray. I hand my camera to my friend Ed and ask him to take pictures of me at the top and on the Chair of Death, knowing that I'll be too far away to be recognizable, but it gives me hope for the future.

When it's my turn, I walk leadenly to the start. I woodenly follow the instructions, my mind feeling as if it's wrapped in a fuzzy sweater. My mouth is cat-litter dry, my tongue thick, and I mumble "okay" to the instructions, but I don't really hear them. Using all ten thumbs, I very clumsily snap the carabiner on my safety harness to the overhead wire and twist the fail-safe lock. One of the instructors asks if I'm all right, because apparently I don't look so well, and I admit how frightened I am. She smiles and says, "It's all right," and tells me that she was scared her first time, too, but that the safety harness has worked every time—"so far." She smiles again.

I look dully at her and say, "I know that here," tapping the small part of my forehead that's not covered by the helmet, "but I don't know it here," grasping my stomach with both hands. I'm feeling nauseous.

"You'll be fine," she says. "Just breathe deeply and don't look down. You'll have fun."

"How do you *not* look down when you're walking on a wire that's an inch thick?" I murmur.

She doesn't answer the unanswerable but simply says, "It's time to go. Good luck; have fun."

I grasp the handrails, take a deep breath to fight the nausea and fear, and step onto the wire. It's very much an out-of-body experience; someone else is doing this, not me. I'm just watching.

To my surprise, the wire is springy, and it snakes a bit as my body weight and foot placement move it. Despite what the instructor said, this is not fun, and as I slowly work my way out on the wire, the ground drops away like a cliff. My head begins to spin, and I get lightheaded; my legs get wobbly, and I can taste my gastric juices. About halfway to the first pole, my legs simply give out, and I sink to my knees. I'm having a full-blown panic attack.

People on the ground start telling me things, asking me things, but I can't really hear them. I have very rarely been pushed to such an edge, and never to such a complete loss of control of my mind and body. I instinctively know that I have nothing left; I'm deeply stuck. So, chin sunk to my chest, crouched on a wire twenty-five feet off the ground, in as helpless a situation as I've ever been in, I pray: "Dear God ... it doesn't have to be pretty, but I cannot ... I cannot do this alone. Please give me the strength I need."

This is it. This is the edge that psychologists such as Carl Jung, philosophers such as Søren Kierkegaard, and spiritual leaders such as John of the Cross, Buddha, and Mahatma Gandhi believe is necessary before true spiritual transformation can happen. This is the personal wilderness that we must submit ourselves to before we can stand before God, spiritually nude, shorn of all pretension, as our most simple selves. J. N. Figgis, an English historian, philosopher, and monk who lived in the nineteenth and twentieth centuries, wrote about finding yourself at this edge:

> Ask yourself for one moment what your feelings have been on the eve of some act involving courage, whether it has been physical courage as it is commonly called, or moral or intellectual.... What has happened to you? If it has really called forth courage, has it not felt something like this?
>
> > I cannot do this. This is too much for me. I shall ruin myself if I take this risk. I cannot take the leap, it's impossible. All of me will be gone if I do this, and I cling to myself.
>
> And then supposing the Spirit has conquered and you have done this impossible thing, do you find afterwards that you possess yourself in a sense that you never had before? That there is more of you? ... So it is throughout life ... You know "nothing ventured nothing won" is true in every hour, it is the fibre of every experience that signs itself into the memory.[2]

"*I cannot do this. This is too much.*" Is this how the Israelites felt when they walked into the desert with Moses? And would they have even started out if they had known the trip was going to last forty years? Is this what Jesus experienced when he was thrown into the desert for forty days of testing and temptation? Is this how centuries of initiates on vision quests have felt when they looked into the unknown chasm of their testing?

Like the Israelites, like Jesus, like initiates on a vision quest, we achieve real learning when we are past the comfortable and into the risky parts of life that force us to our edges. Recognizing how little we control is a first step.

In his book *The Solace of Fierce Landscapes*, Belden Lane writes, "Certain truths can be learned, it seems, only as one is sufficiently emptied, frightened, or confused.... Extremity is the necessary, even normative starting point for understanding the strenuous character of the spiritual life."[3]

Others have voiced similar ideas. The Roman playwright Seneca said in *De Providentia*, "Gold is refined in fire, and acceptable men in the furnace of adversity." The thirteenth-century Sufi poet and mystic Rumi wrote, "This discipline and rough treatment are a furnace to extract the silver from the dross. This testing purifies the gold by boiling the scum away."[4]

In other words, it may not be possible to have testing experiences in any place *but* a wilderness, in a place that pushes us to edges we rarely explore in our normal lives. Only when our human efforts come up short can we learn the important spiritual lesson of complete dependence on God.

RELYING ON GOD

Things get very clear when you are cornered.
—*Chogyam Trungpa (1939–1987),
Tibetan Buddhist meditation master*

As I crouch on that perilous wire, my psalmist's prayer of abject supplication, my fervent request for God's immediate action, is answered. Within five seconds, the nausea ceases, the lightheadedness ends, my legs regain their strength, and I can stand. People yell up encouragement, and I start walking again to the first pole. I am not pretty, or fast, but I'm moving. When I reach the first pole, it feels life-giving, and I hug it shamelessly before I unhook the carabiner and attach it to the next safety wire.

"Thank you, thank you" is all I can muster, for I'm still very shaky and only slightly less frightened. But I can continue, and I slowly work my way, without physical grace (but feeling very filled with grace) to the top level. I don't remember much from the first pole up to the last level, except that looking down didn't terrorize me as much.

At the top level, where we do the teamwork challenge, my partner and I face each other. We talk about how we're going to handle this and begin to negotiate the diabolical, mostly parallel wires, holding on to each other's shoulders with a vice-like grip. After a tense, five-minute crab-scuttling traverse, we arrive at the final platform. And there, waiting for us, is an astounding view of the Pisgah Forest—and the Chair of Death.

Attached to a thick rope, whose other end is attached to a stout brace on a pole that's twenty-five yards downslope, the Chair of Death sits silently in a cradle, its open seat gaping like the maw of a waiting, patient beast. It's painted a sinister matte black, and notches, which have not been painted over, are carved into the top edge of the seat back. We don't ask ...

Fog is rolling quickly up the mountainside as my partner climbs into the chair. He smiles wanly at me while the instructors fit the shoulder harness and lap belt around him, and suddenly he's gone, fast as a clap, dropped completely out of sight. I look over the edge of the platform and see him arcing at insane speed toward the ground—tiny, flashing past the pole, and disappearing into the fog. He looks like a gob of bait at the end of a fishing line that's been cast into milky water, and it seems as if a gigantic "something" has got him, because the line seems to hang straight out in the fog, defying the gravity that should be pulling him back ... until, finally, the line does come back, and my partner swings, as a human pendulum, for about two minutes.

Then it's my turn.

I'm strangely calm about this whole thing. After what I've been through in making my way to this point, I see the Chair of Death as my ticket off this tower of de Sade. It is my chariot of salvation, so I am not especially afraid as I'm strapped in. It doesn't seem very daunting, and I almost welcome it. I'm unconcerned as the chair lurches out of the cradle and rockets downward, then shoots past the people on the ground and into the fog. In fact, I kind of enjoy it, and I almost feel that I'm an observer. As I swing back and forth, I am, simply, relieved.

When I'm released from the chair, everyone who's not on the ropes course congratulates me, and I try to be sincere in my thanks. But I know they don't understand. They think I prevailed through sheer willpower, and they're impressed because word has spread about my boundless fear of heights.

But I know differently. I know how close to total meltdown I had come; I know how utterly reliant on God I'd been. I'd seen myself at the ugly end of desperation; I'd felt how quickly my full bowl of confidence was overturned. My own resources, in which I'd taken such pride for so long, had failed me, and I had been as far over the edge as I ever hope to be.

But in that experience, I discovered that I wasn't alone at the edge. I'd met God there. I'd given lip service to the concept of meeting God at the edge many times, but, naively, I'd always assumed that it was *God's* edge, not mine. My faulty thinking went something like this:

(a) The wilderness—where I've most frequently experienced God's presence—is on the edge of civilization.

(b) The wilderness is a reflection of God's handiwork.

(c) There is a very long tradition from all parts of the world that people go to the wilderness to find God.

If (a), (b), and (c) are true, then (d), there must be some invisible barrier to God around civilized places, so the wilderness is *God's* edge, where God can be engaged.

Not a terribly elegant or well-thought-out rationale, but it worked for me for a time—though it was completely wrong, as I learned. It is when we reach *our* edge, when testing exposes us for what we are and reduces us to our essence, that God can teach us.

SCHOOLMASTER OF LIFE

Suffering [which I prefer to call "testing"] is but another
name for the teaching of experience, which is the parent
of instruction and the schoolmaster of life.

—Horace (65–8 BCE), Roman poet

Many people ask me why I think the wilderness is so effective in
revealing our edges.

My answer usually is this: When we enter the wilderness, we
cross over the physical and spiritual boundaries we know and
expect. For starters, the wilderness usually requires significant physical activity beyond our ordinary routines. We may be called on to
tap into strengths and resources we didn't know we had. That's not
to say that working in our gardens or walking through a city park
can't be physical reminders of God's presence in our lives. But most
often these "civilized wildernesses" will not give us the in-our-gut
experience of God's presence in the way that true immersion in the
wild can. To put it bluntly, we aren't usually sensitive to God's presence if we're in comfortable places because we don't *need* God
when we're comfortable. Instead, our sensitivity to God is much
greater, much more immediate, at the edges where things aren't
comfortable or predictable, where our civilized niceties lose their
grip and are revealed for the generally shallow things they are.

When we enter the wilderness, we enter unfamiliar territory
that is so vast it reminds us that we, these impossibly tiny beings, are
not the Masters of the Universe—but that we are in the presence of
the one who is. We're constantly reminded that nature is larger and
far more timeless than we are, that it is something beyond our control that we can neither create nor improve. It's in these times that
we come to realize both our own finitude and God's infinitude.

The problem is that, while most of us understand that we cannot get this kind of true wilderness immersion in the city—in the
Bible, for example, how often is God encountered in the city?

(almost never)—we civilized folks are simply not stampeding to wild places. Neither were Jesus's disciples. Jesus spent almost his entire ministry at the edge—or over it—of Jewish civilization, usually at the edges of the wilderness. He frequently took his very reluctant disciples outside their comfort zones, into the lands of the Gentiles, crossing both physical and metaphorical boundaries. He took them across the Sea of Galilee to the swine-herding lands of the Gerasenes to heal a Gentile possessed by demons (Luke 8:26–39). He took them across the northern border of Israel into Tyre to affirm the faith of a Syrophoenician woman and to cure her daughter (Matthew 15:21–28). He fed a multitude on the foreign side of a lake (Mark 8:1–10). Consistently, Jesus dragged his disciples from the comfort of the known to the edges of the unfamiliar and unknown, to places where their understanding of God was opened, beyond their usual experience and beyond their culture.[5] He pushed his, and their, boundaries by being on the edge.

Yet, knowing in our hearts that the benefits of leaving civilization for a while may be legion, many of us still avoid the wilderness because it seems too challenging. So we backpedal like crazy sometimes—maybe often—because getting close to the Divine is a scary prospect. But in the same way that birds simply must answer the call to migrate, despite all the dangers that lie in the journey, we also have that instinctive imperative. We are driven by an urge to both go deeper and, paradoxically, move closer to the edge where we can meet both our better selves and God. Time spent in wild places enables us to do both. In spiritual, physical, and psychological ways, the wilderness grounds us by setting us free from our self-imposed limitations.

Here's how one woman chose to move to her edge. Like me, she had a fear of heights, but nevertheless she chose to hike down the narrow trails of the mile-high walls of the Grand Canyon. Different place, different person, and different context, but a familiar coming-to-the-edge experience:

I was scared to death ... the whole time we were traveling down, this fear was right below the surface. At points there would be a wall, and I would say to myself, "I'm going down." My biggest fear was if my pack hit the wall, I would fall over the edge. So it really was a survival thing for me. I cried a few times and just had to stop, and didn't know if I could go on. But the feeling when I finally reached the [bottom] was overwhelming! I mean, to know I had succeeded was so empowering.... I proved to myself that I could do some things that I didn't think I could do. And through the pain and fear, I discovered my body was stronger than I had thought it was.[6]

Experiences like this, when we confront our limits and find ourselves wanting, change us. It certainly changed the prophet Elijah when he was fleeing for his life. He "went a day's journey into the wilderness" and simply "sat down under a broom tree." He was at the end of his endurance, willing to die rather than go on: "It is enough; now, O Lord, take away my life, for I am no better than my ancestors" (1 Kings 19:4). But God's angel came to him, revived him with care, food, and drink, and told him to go on—which he did, for "forty days and forty nights"—to Mount Horeb (19:8).

Through doing something "impossible," many of us have had the spiritual experience of finding something inside ourselves that we never expected, and the affirmation that we have expanded our lives in the process. Whether we seek wilderness in nature, or encounter one of life's wildernesses—such as addiction, prison, sickness, dying, aging, divorce, or job loss—these experiences at the edge can show us once again how vulnerable we are. As W. Scott Olsen wrote in his essay "An Advent Nature," "In a reversal of perception, we can now look at wild places as places of healing, and of relative safety and peace, whereas civilization leads often to chaos and brokenness. 'In Wilderness,' said Thoreau, 'is the preservation of the world.'"[7]

But there are other wildernesses, as we know.

In *Hamlet*, act 1, scene 5, Shakespeare wisely tells us that "there are more things in heaven and earth, Horatio, / than are dreamt of in your philosophy," and in the same vein there are more wildernesses than we can dream of in our own realities. On-the-edge experiences don't all occur in the wilderness of nature. The most painful wildernesses are often far from the mountains or streams, but are, instead, in the profoundly scraping process of living. Having been through some of them myself, I'd say that those life wildernesses often take a bit of detachment—and time—to see the good through the hurt, as the man in the following paragraphs describes.

The worst parts about prison are the humiliation, the total loss of personal identity, having no control at all over my daily existence, and the prison-encouraged belief that I'd resigned my status as a human being. It is a wide-awake nightmare.

For the first ten days I was held in a five-by-eight cell with another man. There was no electricity, no light, and no information either from the outside or about what was going to happen to me next.

I had nothing to read or do. Food was pushed through a hole in the door. I got outside one hour a week, and I could shower and shave only once a week at the system's discretion. Three times a day we were subjected to full-body pat downs and cavity searches. When it got dark, I went to bed. All my bodily functions were on full view to my cellmate, and his to me. Modesty was nonexistent, and with nothing to do, day or night, my thoughts went to dark and desolate places. I was as low as I'd ever been in my life, which, at that point, had no point.

Things improved slightly when I was transferred to a more modern prison, but a cage is still a cage, and my world was still confined to the walls of my cell block. Inmates beat each other senseless over meager personal belongings, which had come to define their identity. For many of these men, prison is a better life than they had outside. But the wilderness of prison has no beauty; there is never a quiet moment, even at night, and we're never, ever alone.

In the midst of this horror something began happening. When we're at our lowest point people often turn to God, and that's what I did. I've always given lip service to God and God's love of the oppressed and imprisoned, but now it took on new and very personal meaning. I stopped saying the rote prayers I'd been taught and began praying with personal urgency, and it slowly brought me peace. As I combined meditation with prayer, I had some experiences of grace in the midst of turmoil, and a phrase began running through my mind: "You have nothing to fear; I am with you always."

I began to feel forgiven. I began to feel, for the first time in my life, that I had a personal relationship with God, not just an abstract one. As the feeling grew I knew that if I could hold up under the prison culture, then with God's help, I could withstand nearly anything.

Now that I'm out, I realize I learned some important things in that valley of the shadow. I laugh at life's—and my— silliness, and I take both a lot less seriously. I'm comfortable now knowing that I'm a fallible, unfinished work and that I'm truly loved, in spite of myself, not only by God but by the friends and the woman who stood by me, despite the hurt I caused them all. I realize how much I had taken that for granted. I no longer allow the world to define who I am ... and I am truly happier now than I've been in my entire adult life. Prison had its own strange/wonderful gifts to offer me, though I don't recommend the experience.

—Name withheld to preserve anonymity

Some remarkably wise person said, "Life is so hard because it gives us the test first, then the lesson." Nearly anyone with some mileage on his or her life knows that that's true, and this book is filled with examples. In some universal way, we all have our own "prisons," or wildernesses, that take us to the test, followed by the lesson. And in that test on the edge, beyond comfort, God meets us with the possibility of life-changing transformation.

QUESTIONS FOR REFLECTION

• Think of a time when you made a choice to do something unpredictable, something beyond your experience or social/cultural/religious boundaries. How did that experience impact you?

• Have you ever had to face something that you feared greatly? How did you feel? What helped you face it?

• Think of a time when you felt as if you had no control over a situation, and the only thing you could do was to rely on God. How did that feel? What did you learn from that?

• Do you think it is true that we have to go into a "wilderness" to have a deeper connection with God? Or a truer connection to life? How might an intentional wilderness experience change you? Or, if you've had an intentional wilderness experience, what was its effect on your life?

• What "prisons" have you been in, and what pulled you through? What strengths and weaknesses did you discover about yourself, and how have those experiences impacted your life? Can you see, in retrospect, any gifts from that experience? Any lessons? Do you think you could have learned those lessons in an easier environment?

HEALING WATERS
THE WILDERNESS LEADS US TO SOLITUDE AND SILENCE SO WE CAN KNOW OURSELVES AND GOD.

MAGNIFICENT AND SCARY

> Language ... has created the word *loneliness* to express the
> pain of being alone. And it has created the word *solitude*
> to express the glory of being alone.
> —*Paul Johannes Tillich*, The Eternal Now

None of us have ever been in a wilderness as untouched as this. It is so utterly wild that the only trails we find—and they are very few—have been made by caribou and last only ten to fifteen yards. It is so isolated that we may be the first people ever to cross some of these especially remote and difficult mountain passes. Here in the Northern Talkeetna Mountains of Alaska, all the world's greatest adjectives are miniaturized by the scenery, and by our physical and spiritual experiences.

Places like Alaska require time alone, time to think, time to reflect, time to absorb. And in Alaska there is so much to absorb because it is huge in every way—stunning, almost incomprehensible in its vastness.

The problem with Alaska, phenomenal as it is, is that it is grizzly heavy country. We're here in July and August on a back-packing trip, but May and June were drier than usual, so the berries aren't as plentiful as they should be, and the bears aren't as well fed as they want to be. Our concern, of course, is that they will come after our food, and we'll be in the way. Added to our concern is knowing that the first snows are only six weeks away. The bears certainly sense it, for it is with great deliberation that they are trying to lay in their stores of fat for their long hibernation. At lower elevations we frequently see their beds and the remains of their kill, so our rule of thumb is to always be in groups of three, preferably four. (To our knowledge, there have never been grizzly attacks on a group of four or more.)

So, no solitude. None. Not even when we go to relieve ourselves. We have to abandon any sense of modesty and hike off in a foursome to do our business, always at least two hundred yards from our tents and the kitchen area, which are separated from each other by at least one hundred yards for the same bear reasons. We prefer that the bears raid our kitchen rather than our tents with us in them, making of us what those with darker humors called "bear burritos."

To help prevent that possibility, we carefully brush our teeth and thoroughly wash our hands and faces before sleeping to erase any food smell. No toothpaste, no lotions of any kind can be near the tents. Truthfully, the risk is relatively low, but smart wilderness travel dictates very cautionary measures—especially around unpredictable grizzlies—and since we are easily seventy-five miles from any civilization, and the weather can often hamper speedy air rescue, prudence seems, well ... prudent. We want great stories to tell back home—but not survivor stories. However, the lack of any time alone gets to some people and reduces one woman to tears on several occasions. We give her tent time whenever we can.

We all want a bit of solitude from time to time. Yet, for the most part, people in our culture do not spend time alone on purpose. Perhaps we never did, because we're social animals by nature, meant to be in community. While living in community certainly has its obvious advantages, along the way we have also lost something vitally important: the benefit of intentional solitude.

Humans have always found solitude both a magnificent and a scary thing—often simultaneously. Magnificent because it is solely ours, and the possibilities for enrichment and growth seem endless, including the chance to contemplate some of life's deepest questions: Who am I? Why am I here? Where is God in all this? Where do God and I figure in each other's plans? Whose life am I living, and why?

And scary, for precisely the same reasons.

In solitude we are not lonely, perhaps, but we are alone.

Loneliness, in contrast, is a wilderness of its own because it's the absence of being with others, with ourselves, or with God. It implies an emptiness. But solitude is different from loneliness; it offers the promise of not only a core connection with ourselves but also with God:

> *The ability to just get away and be alone, and to listen and observe, and maybe think that it's God's thoughts that are going through my mind … it's just very profound.*
>
> —Bryan C. Abbott, on a canoe trip
> on the Wisconsin River

But, still, we're not used to being alone. We're not trained or encouraged to be alone, so we don't know what to do with solitude—especially when it means that we're also not surrounded by the familiar things of our highly barnacled, overstimulated lives. We're at a loss: What do I do now?! No TV, no computer, no music, no meetings, no phones, no PDAs, no books, no people.

Type A personalities, particularly, feel that spending twenty-four hours alone doing "nothing" is a waste of time.

But what if we reframe that statement (or complaint) with a "yes but": Yes ... but ... we're "wasting" time with God. This is what the Desert Fathers and Mothers told the Type A's of their times. Nearly every religious tradition teaches that there is much to be gained from intentional solitude undertaken with no other agenda than to spend time alone with God and oneself, searching with heart for both. The solitary spiritual quest in the wilderness is not confined to select cultural or religious traditions. It is an honored and seminal part of the Judeo-Christian, Buddhist, Native American, Hindu, aboriginal, Shinto, and Inuit traditions, among others.

Like the American Indians, the Inuit in the Arctic coastal areas of Alaska, Siberia, the Northwest Territories of Canada, Nunavut, Labrador, and Greenland have a solitary vision quest tradition that uses the extreme forces of nature to shape the spiritual lives of the young men in their small ice-bound communities. As the Inuit shaman Igjugarjuk said, "All true wisdom is only to be learned ... out in the great solitudes."[1]

Buddhists also place a high value on solitude, knowing that the Buddha was on a spiritual quest for many years, roaming as a starving ascetic before sitting under a Bodhi tree in the ancient sacred forests of Uruvela in northern India, seeking perfect enlightenment. Appropriately, most Buddhist retreat centers are in natural settings—forest or mountains—because Buddhists have understood since well before the birth of Jesus that solitude in natural places opens people to insights that are nearly impossible in more crowded places.

In the seventh century, Muhammad sought the wilderness solitude of a cave on Mount Hira, outside of Mecca, as he received God's word that later became the Qur'an. Islam, however, approaches desert solitude, and living there, with caution: "It is

124

necessary to 'realize' the desert of spiritual solitude before the sole existent being, God. But it is dangerous to actually take abode in the desert."[2] They understand the risk of developing the arrogance of self-reliance and the cult of self-absorption. In spite of that, however, Muslims also recognize that the desert, both through its nature and its symbols, brings human beings closer to God.

In perhaps the most famous example of seeking solitude, Jesus went to the wilderness in a constant ebb and flow, moving from complete immersion in his public ministry, then intentionally retreating to the wilderness to get recharged by God so that he could resume his ministry. He knew—as we know, but often try to ignore—that we need spiritual food as much as we need physical food to be healthy and to live a full, abundant life.

The ritual of intentional solitude as it has been practiced in various forms for centuries, by people across the globe, hasn't lost any of its power, as contemporary pilgrim David Douglas relates in his essay "Inviting Solitude":

> I spent scores of nights under the stars before I had an inkling that the country offered more than a picturesque landscape. Something else was happening here, something that promised to alter how I viewed my relationship to God. I'm not sure if anything but the outlines of that pride-splintering sense of vulnerability would have been apparent to me had I not entered the wilderness, at long last, alone.[3]

"At long last, alone." On the pre-trip questionnaire for Renewal in the Wilderness trips, one of the questions asks, "What concerns do you have about your trip?"

Often the response is, "I'm more afraid of the solo time than I am of the animals or the physical challenges."

That's significant information because part of every Renewal in the Wilderness trip includes a period of intentional solitude. On weeklong trips the solo lasts for twenty-four hours. We plan this for a point in the trip when people have acquired enough wilderness skills, and will be comfortable enough in the environment, to be on solo with competence and in safety. Some people look forward to this time; most are concerned about it.

Our minds may "know" that wilderness solitude will allow us to spend important time with ourselves and with God, but that doesn't stop us from being apprehensive. Yet, without solitude, we will miss one of the great gifts of the wilderness as David Rensberger tells us in his essay "Deserted Places":

> In order to become fully human ... we need to spend time without other humans. The great gift of deserted country to us is solitude, the chance to be alone before God. This gift may also be the desert's greatest terror, however. It is not only the possibility of perishing without food or shelter, it is the sheer emptiness of a deserted place that frightens us so badly.... We are left by ourselves, and suddenly we are faced with the question of who that self really is.... The desert lacks everything except the opportunity to know God.[4]

GOING SOLO

> The crops of the wilderness have always been its spiritual values—silence and solitude, a sense of awe and gratitude—able to be harvested by any traveler who visits.
> —*Belden Lane*, The Solace of Fierce Landscapes

Three years after my trip to Alaska, I'm backpacking with a small group in the Absoroka-Beartooth Mountains of Montana (*absoroka* means "crow" in the Crow Indian language). Unlike the Alaska trip, there will be real opportunities to be without other people. We're here for ten days, and everything we'll need we're carrying; there will be no resupply. So my pack is monstrously heavy, but it's the price I pay willingly for the chance to be here and to spend time alone at some point in our trip. The others are looking forward to some wilderness solitude as well.

As it was in Alaska, there are grizzlies in Montana, but far fewer. Our greater worry is black bears, but they're not as aggressive as brown bears, so we feel that periods of solitude will be safe enough. As we work our way into the backcountry, the scenery from every vantage point is beyond sublime, but it is also very different from that of Alaska. Montana is Big Sky Country, but it feels more intimate, closer, than Alaska felt. Every way we look seems like one postcard view after the other, but this is the real thing.

After a tough, huffing climb up a fifteen-degree trail at nine thousand feet, we reach a valley where alpine meadows open up to valley floors covered in grass and lupine, interspersed with extravagant swatches of buttercups, with winding streams of cold mountain water, and pines and aspens that rim the valley like the semicircle on a monk's tonsured head. At dawn or dusk we sometimes see elk and deer, always watchful, always stately, and we know there are also moose at these altitudes. As we do with bears, we hope to see a moose, but at a distance because they are also quite dangerous.

Surrounding all of this impossible beauty is the equally impossible beauty of the young spire-y peaks that come to such sharp points that we wonder aloud how the snow is able to stick to them. We understand now why they're called the Beartooth Mountains. Clouds flirt in and about the peaks like a slow-motion weaver's shuttle, and at times envelop them in moving oceans of cotton. If there is heaven on earth, it looks like this, and we can begin to understand why even starchy theologians such as sixteenth-century John Calvin would say, "You cannot in one glance survey this most vast and beautiful system of the universe, in its wide expanse, without being completely overwhelmed by the boundless force of its brightness."[5]

The days go on like this, hiking through this "boundless force of brightness," one place of beauty leading to another, to another, as we burrow further into the wilderness. The deeper we go, the fewer people we see until, after the third day, we see no one else until we reach the trailhead at the end of the trip. We're beyond the areas reached by day hikers and weekenders, and the terrain gets more rugged—and more stunning. We're getting into the routine of our days, hardening to the rigors, adapting to the seven- to eleven-thousand-foot altitudes, loving the challenges, anticipating how good camp food tastes after a day on the trail.

On the sixth day, we decide that we're in the right place for our solos, so late in the morning we set up a base camp and then choose our individual sites. They're all out of view of each other, but within whistle shot for safety. We select our food, take our tarps in case of rain, and pack our sleeping pads and sleeping bags, rain gear, and enough clothing to stay warm. We make sure we have enough water, and our journals and pens. After lunch, we review safety protocols and renew a promise that we won't stray more than twenty-five yards from our sites in case we need to be found quickly. Then we're off to our campsites for the next twenty-four hours.

My site is at the edge of a vast mountain meadow that is apparently too high for the fierce display of wildflowers we had seen at lower elevations, but it is filled with waving tall, brown grasses that have an earthy, sweet smell. The meadow drops off to a valley that I can't see, but abruptly on the other side, and in jolting contrast to the gentleness of the meadow, rise three massive mountain chunks of granite that look as if God simply dropped them there and then chiseled the tops to look like thick, gray canine teeth with snow at the top. From my vantage point these mountains look like an impenetrable wall as they rise another three thousand feet above me.

I find an ancient lodge pole pine five feet in diameter that snapped about four feet off the ground in a long-ago windstorm but never separated from the main trunk. It is almost horizontal to the ground. I try with all my strength to push it off its base, but I can't budge it—which is good, because my hope is to camp beneath it, using it as a ridge pole from which to suspend my tarp. I sit for an hour by the stump looking for ants (and ground-squirrel holes), which often have nests at the base of trees, but find nothing, so it's confirmed: This is where I'll sleep. I set up the tarp, making sure, again, that there are no dead trees nearby that could fall on me during the night if a mighty wind kicks up. I inflate my mattress, fluff up my sleeping bag (putting my pack over the mouth to keep critters out), and then scout the forest behind my tree.

Keeping to my promise of a twenty-five-yard perimeter, that still gives me about thirty minutes' worth of exploration. The old coniferous forest is filled with many lodge pole pines—some dead, many living, but all strong and straight and spiraling—and also Engelman spruce and some Douglas fir. The needles they have shed for decades carpet the ground and make it springy and silent to walk on; the air is laden with their beautiful pine smell. Squirrels are everywhere, cheeky as hell, cussing me out for the intrusion on their territory.

Having explored as much of my site as possible, I take my camp chair out into the meadow to sit down with nature, and just be. This is what I've been waiting for. My goal is to clear my mind of as much noise as possible, to sink metaphorical roots from my butt into the ground, and become one with this environment to see what happens.

I have my journal, I have my camera and binoculars and water, and I'm willing to be—*hoping* to be—overwhelmed by a moment of divine presence. I think of Thomas Merton's line from his *Thoughts in Solitude*: "As soon as you are really alone, you are with God." But even if nothing remarkably spiritual happens, I'm truly happy to be here.

And so I sit for four hours without moving, waiting. For whatever. I'd love to see some large herbivores amble across the meadow and not even notice me (I admit I'm less anxious to see large carnivores ambling nearby), but it doesn't happen. I watch the shadow play of the clouds as they cross the granite chunk mountains and the meadow, and I marvel at the sound of the wind as it hustles through the trees, then goes silent as it crosses the empty meadow, and then gets vocal again in the trees on the meadow's other side. It's like listening to an invisible velvet train as it rushes into a tunnel, goes silent, and becomes "visible" to the ears again as it punches out the other side.

I've had enough solo experiences to know that there's a predictable rhythm to a lengthy period of solitude, and I'm hoping to avoid what I've always encountered before: At a certain point, my busyness mode, or my need to be entertained, kicks in and says, "Okay ... I'm getting kind of bored here, so now what do I do?"

And there's never an answer other than, "Do nothing—just be."

I remind myself of what a woman on another trip wrote: "It's when I take that time out and just let myself 'be,' without doing or acting, that I nourish my soul."[6]

Still, and predictably, I try to fill the time with things to *do*. But I can only journal so much, I can look through the binoculars only so much, I can watch the clouds and listen to the wind just so much, and there aren't any large animals sauntering past to entertain me ... so now what? I can pay all the lip service I want to the glories of solitude, but here's where, as the commercials say, the rubber meets the road.

Dear God! What do I do with my time, my hands ... *my mind?* I'm not at all sure I know me, or even like me, but now I'm stuck with me for twenty-four hours. Can I go that long in silence?

But that's exactly why I'm here: I want to get past the boredom and go deeper. I want to stop listening to the rattly noises of my mind and listen instead to the much deeper sounds of my heart. Fortunately, by the time I had come to these Absaroka-Beartooth Mountains, I had learned about *apophatic* prayer, or prayer without words. Apophatic prayer seems tailor-made for wild landscapes that leave you asthmatic for words. It is based on the belief that prayer *with* words is automatically limited because words themselves have limits and can't express either what's in the heart or the scope of God ... even if we had a glimmer of the scope of God. Apophatic prayer suggests that, in complete mental and bodily silence, we can begin to be part of the depth of creation because we are open—as we're able, without judgment—to what God puts before us. In the apophatic state, our entire being *is* the prayer. And in that state we can become connected to God.

Sitting in that mountain meadow, I enter quickly into apophatic prayer, and I feel rooted in the ground, to all the mountains that surround me; to the sky, the wind, and the sunlight; and to whatever animals might come by. I can hear the air ruffing through the wings of birds that fly over my head. The peace and sense of well-being is almost overwhelming, and time—my time, at least—stands still.

Melting into apophatic prayer is not easy to do, and until this experience I'd never been able to maintain it for more than a few minutes. It is trance-like and so profoundly peaceful that I think this must be what Transcendental Meditation strives for. Belden Lane said it well: "Our only way out of the desert is to go deeper into it, beyond the breakdown of language to the 'still point' where God meets us in emptiness."[7]

And in our emptiness we can be filled, for there is room, now, for God.

THE HEALING PROCESS

> True silence is the rest of the mind, and is to the spirit
> what sleep is to the body, nourishment and refreshment.
> —*William Penn (1645–1718)*

Solitude. And silence.

The two are nearly conjoined twins, for they move together even though they're separate. They beat with the same heart, pump the same blood, nourish the same body, and exhale the same warm and moist life. Much is made in the Hebrew and Christian scriptures about the breath of God. In Genesis, for example, God's breath swept over the unformed earth. In Acts, Jesus breathed God's breath on each of his disciples. So on Renewal in the Wilderness trips we do meditation exercises that focus on God's breath. Solitude and silence may be the bearers of God's breath for us.

Much of the value of the wilderness experience is being immersed in the healing embrace of silence and solitude. I've had amazing experiences of God's presence during solos, when life is reduced to its essentials and I am surrounded by God's creation and opened to God's voice. It is in these times of silent solitude, in places like my isolated meadow in Montana, that soul-bending experiences occur most frequently and most intensely for many people.

The words of backpacker Tom Shealey evocatively describe this experience:

> I need such places [great unbound swaths of wilderness] because there the stillness descends and wraps itself around me like an old friend come to comfort me.... I want to hide, if just temporarily, where the air is heavy with silence and heal so that I come back whole again.... Solitude stirs a watchfulness that sharpens your senses and makes you alert.... In the stillness, emotions surface. Your self-awareness is heightened, as is your creativity, sensitivity, sympathy, compassion and empathy. Because there are no noisy distractions to hide behind, the silent land becomes your mirror, where you meet yourself face-to-face and find the truth—about yourself and about the world around you. It's where you clearly hear the voice of reason that can safely and accurately guide you from within. When it comes to choosing life's paths, the heart knows the way, but it whispers and can be heard only in the stillness of the wilds.[8]

You may have heard the line "Nowadays most men lead lives of noisy desperation," attributed to James Thurber, the famous cartoonist and humorist of the mid-1900s. Thurber's statement is a parody of Thoreau's saying that most people live lives of quiet desperation, but both sayings, in their own ways, are probably right. I suspect that we live quietly desperate, but surrounded with noise to mute our own thoughts and voices, and to fill our emptiness.

How addicted are we to constant sound? I know many people—myself *sometimes* included—who turn on the TV or radio the first thing in the morning and as soon as they come home from work, and leave it on until they go to bed. My sister has a timer on her TV so she can fall asleep to the "reassuring" noise but not be awakened by it later. My daughter hates to run without her MP3 player because running isn't entertainment enough. My children are always astounded that my wife and I don't constantly have music on to overcome the silence. If Thurber's satiric humor sounds as if it still hits the mark, consider how much more noise we have now in the twenty-first century than when he wrote his parody in the fifties!

I think Mother Teresa was exactly right when she said, "God ... cannot be found in noise and restlessness. God is the friend of silence. See how nature—trees, flowers, grass—grows in silence; see the stars, the moon, and the sun, how they move in silence." It's also telling that in both the Hebrew and Christian Bibles, God's revelation and personal interaction with human beings is almost always in quiet places, never in the cities and rarely in crowds.

This news is old news—ancient, actually—and is the cornerstone of many religions, but we need reminding today more than ever. In an important study published by the *Journal of Environmental Psychology*, two groups of women who went to two very different wilderness areas (the Boundary Waters Canoe Area in northern Minnesota and the Grand Canyon of northern Arizona) described the impact of the solitude and silence of the wilderness on their spiritual inspiration:

> It was ... wonderful ... when I could go off on my own.... I felt more connected to myself and even to the other people on the trip after ... these ... periods of solitude. [B]eing alone is when I found my center.[9]

> [In my times of solitude] I noticed more, I felt more.... I felt more connected to myself and even to the other people on the trip.... Being alone is when I found my center.... It was like returning to a place deep inside me, and visiting an older, wiser me ... even though I felt young and vitally alive too.... It made me feel like I had a home again.[10]

The authors of the study reported that people found the wilderness "incredibly useful to engage in more contemplative and self-reflective thinking, as it seemed to help them maintain their own mental, spiritual, and emotional well-being."[11] Most of the women said that their periods of solitude rejuvenated them and "gave them a renewed sense of hope about the challenges that were waiting for them back at home."[12]

On the many Renewal in the Wilderness trips I've led, women and men describe very similar experiences of the grounding effects of solitude:

> *On our twenty-four hour solo I had time to do a lot of reflection. I was not near the river, but I found a vantage point on the edge of a lagoon where I could sit in the sand and see the moon between some trees. As it got high enough, it was reflected in the small lagoon; as I watched the reflection I thought about God's expectation that each of us reflect God's teachings. When my life is chaotic, like the moon's reflection distorted by the ripples of the water, my reflection will not look*

as much like God; it also will be distorted. In solitude I can make sense of this, and hear my heart.

—Barbara Oakes, on a canoe trip
on the Wisconsin River

I have never known faith, not in others and not in myself. And it is faith I have come here to find, in solitude. I am so fatigued by all the hurting souls I see, and I am always trying to find faith in others and harvest the good in others, only nothing I try, or at least, nothing I feel I have tried, is good enough.... I always do things halfway, but today I will go to the top of the visible rise and take myself to meet my faith....

[Then, later in the journal, after a successful hike up a steep mountain trail:] It's wonderful to be quiet, self-directed, unburdened and moving.... It had taken two full days to let go, to turn it over. I had found some aspects of faith on the hikes. Quiet places in my heart which I had not heard in decades.

—Edward Ravine, on a wilderness trip
to Big Cottonwood Canyon in Utah

Silence and solitude in the wilderness have an enormous capacity to begin a healing process in people who have been hurt. I've been privileged to have people on my trips who began to recover from the darkness of divorce, death of loved ones, death of parents and siblings, job loss, and other types of pain (too many to count) because their experiences opened them to a kind of healing that they'd not found in civilized settings.

One woman on a Boundary Waters trip was suffering the heartbreak of a failing marriage, and in the silence and solitude of her trip, she was able to sort out the issues that were poisoning her relationship, and she found the strength to believe—and act on that belief—that the marriage could be saved. Her marriage is today both stable and happy, and is a perfect example of using God's wilderness to heal in a personal wilderness.

A man whose father and brother had recently been killed in an automobile accident was able, for the first time since the accident, to find some perspective and some healing. His trip to the Boundary Waters was the beginning of peace.

A woman on an October trip on the Wisconsin River had lost her husband earlier in the year. It was a sudden, completely unexpected death; they'd been soul partners as well as business partners, and she was devastated. Her pain was relentless; her tears and anguish were always just at eye level. She said, "I wish I believed in God so I could blame him for this." Her depression seemed bottomless, and nothing she'd tried had helped. But on our trip with four other people, who were generous with their support of someone in tremendous pain, in the simplicity and sanctuary of that wilderness setting, she began to feel that perhaps there was still life for her after all, that she could find the strength to continue, and that the pain would eventually subside. She even began to think that there might be a God after all, and a loving one at that, as reflected in the caring of others.

A colleague of mine, suffering profoundly from the death of a mentor and good friend, found her experience on the Wisconsin River to be the place where her healing could begin:

> The trip came at a time when I was grieving the death of my best friend, who had died after a long struggle with cancer. During the final year of his life, I had been his daily caregiver. As I faced my grief, I realized my body was craving the kind of wilderness challenge that my soul had just been through, and that my soul was craving a place of solitude in which to work through the lingering grief. Having been to Israel several times, I would have imagined that wilderness place would be near the Jordan River, not on the Wisconsin River.
>
> Setting up and breaking camp, preparing meals, and paddling the canoe with various partners: each of these tasks presented opportunities for service, negotiation, compromise, and

136

growth. These things drew me out of myself, and the two amaz-
ing thunderstorms we encountered helped me understand my
place in all of this.

In the midst of such company, there was also solitude:
walking the beach in the early morning, basking in the sun on a
sandbar in the afternoon after a hard day's paddle, swimming in
the river at sunset. Each of these moments offered its own peace
and grace, and drew me to the certain knowledge that the sun
would shine again.

This brief time in the wilderness was a resting place in my
navigation through the larger wilderness of grief, a time of facing
my own limits and coming closer to the face of God, a time of
healing and true renewal.

—Rev. Stephanie Perdew, on a canoe trip
on the Wisconsin River

Most people experience the solitude of the wilderness as a time of
letting go and renewal, a "furnace of transformation," as theologian
Henri Nouwen so succinctly described it in *The Way of the Heart.*

For some, however, the solitude of the wilderness is a place of
struggle, where they wrestle with temptations, or engage in one-
on-one combat with their own demons.

The classic poem "Hiawatha" by Henry Wadsworth Longfellow
offers a good example. Hiawatha wrestled many times with the
Great Spirit until Hiawatha was strong enough and worthy to
receive what the Great Spirit had to teach.

In the Hebrew Bible, Jacob physically wrestled with God in
the wilderness of Peniel and fought God to a stalemate. Then God
said to Jacob, "You shall no longer be called Jacob, but Israel, for
you have striven with God and with humans, and have prevailed"
(Genesis 32:28).

Throughout the forty years of their desert wanderings, the
Israelites wrestled with their many demons, including polytheism,
when they said to Moses's brother, Aaron, "Come, make gods for

us, who shall go before us," and then they made a golden calf to worship (Exodus 32:1).

Jesus, too, went into the wilderness and was tempted for forty days and nights, with promises of all the worldly power and luxuries the devil could command.

Adam and Eve, in their innocence, were confronted with temptation and lost; Jesus—innocent as a dove, yet wily as a serpent—wrestled with temptation and won. I have wrestled—and continue to wrestle—both with my relationship with God and (when I get cynical) with the temptation not to believe. This "demon wrestling" has happened to me many times, and not just in the wilderness. It is in the wilderness, however, that answers become most clear to me, and it was there that I learned the only way I could win with God was to lose to God.

Times of solitary soul-searching are important for all of us, though our desert may not resemble the harsh landscape where God approached so many in the Bible. Our time of solitude and renewal may simply involve turning off the TV, or getting away from normal routines, or finding ways to get away from our normal lives of "doing" into lives of "being." Try taking a slow, Type B walk through a park, with no agenda except to be available; spend some idle time loafing along a beach; stop and really smell some flowers or budding bushes and draw their sweet smell deep into your lungs. If you already walk for solitude and exercise, walk your normal route in reverse: you'll see familiar things quite differently.

However or wherever you can, create some opportunities to be alone and quiet, and to get as connected to nature as possible, because it is God's crucible to do some serious wrestling and healing. Seeking solitude and silence are not mainstream impulses, and to seek either of them is neither convenient nor easy. But if you've acquired some of life's battle scars, the distance and perspective of places "at the edge" will help you see the gifts in those experiences. I like the way John Muir put it: "Everybody needs beauty as well as bread, places to play in and pray in, where nature may heal and give strength to body and soul."

This is serious work. Your life, and proper maintenance of it, requires some serious attention to allow it to sing. In the same way an airplane falls to the ground if it's not properly maintained, so do we. And one of our best maintenance programs lies in wild, quiet places, in solitude.

QUESTIONS FOR REFLECTION

- When you think of being totally alone, what images arise for you? What feelings?

- Keep a five-day "sound journal." Be especially aware of the sounds around you, and make notes as the days progress. Include the amount of time you spend in sound and the amount of time in silence. How addicted are you to sound? What sounds are with you almost constantly during the day? What sounds do you add for entertainment, for comfort, as a defense against boredom?

- Give yourself a twenty-four-hour period this week that is as sound-free as possible. Keep a journal of your feelings and reactions.

- Have you ever sought out an extended period of intentional solitude? What was your experience? What did you discover about yourself? About your life? About God? If you haven't experienced "solo time," can you imagine doing so? What would your hopes for such a time be?

- Plan a time this week when you can create a period of solitude, even if it's only for an hour in a garden or park, or in a room in which you don't feel compelled to do something.

Even if you can't get to a wilderness for a week, silence and solitude still have many gifts to offer.

• Is there some hurt or struggle you are currently dealing with in your life? Consider how solitude might help you feel more grounded by allowing space for some perspective. Is there a step you could take toward making an extended period of silence and solitude a reality?

NOTES

8

THE RAPTURE OF BEING ALIVE
THE WILDERNESS OPENS US
TO THE TRANSCENDENT.

PERFECT PITCH

It is not so much for its beauty that the forest makes a
claim upon [our] hearts, as for that subtle something, that
quality of air that emanates from old trees, that so won-
derfully changes and renews a weary spirit.

—*Robert Louis Stevenson (1850–1894)*

On the day after our solo experiences in the Beartooths of
Montana, we are hiking the upper withers of Grass Mountain, trying to reach its eleven-thousand-foot peak and be off the summit
before the daily lightning storms begin. I am carrying a seventy-
pound pack up a boulder field, focusing my steps carefully so I
don't fall into the holes between boulders, testing the stability of
each boulder before I commit to it to be sure my weight won't shift
its balance point. It's exacting work that keeps me very present to
the moment. The sun is brilliant and new in the east, but to the
west the bolls of gray/white cloud are beginning to move in, scouted
first by tendrils of fog, like a climbing vine seeking purchase on a

trellis. We are at about ten thousand feet and breathing hard in the sparse air as we move as quickly as safe footing will allow. As we hike east, up into the sunshine, we're slowly being caught by the fog at our backs.

In the midst of our climb, on the border between brilliant sunlight and cloud, I begin to feel an immense sense of peace, contentment at my center like a gentle tide that envelops me with warm, comforting water, and I intuitively know that there is no place on earth I'd rather be at this moment. I feel in perfect pitch with the universe, as if I am walking with the holy—even, in some measure, that *I* am holy. I'm experiencing something sublimely transcendent through the physical.

Bliss and *grace* are the only two words that come even close to naming what I was feeling then. Though I didn't write the following statement, I easily could have: "I was happy to be in the forest. I had the feeling that I was part of nature, and that I was experiencing life ... in its purest form. I felt truly content.... I was much more in tune with the world and life."[1]

Two years later on a Boundary Waters canoe trip, I had a similar experience, again experiencing the transcendent through the physical. The day had been crisp and iridescent since sunrise, and the sun was now high overhead. It bounced off the crests of the tiny waves, making the lake seem as if it were nature's disco ball. As we canoed toward a narrow channel leading to another lake, the shore on both sides became progressively closer, pinching us toward a narrow opening framed on either side with tall, solitary pine trees.

As we approached the gap, which was so tight that only one canoe at a time could go through, I was overcome with that same sense of profound well-being, of bliss, of universal connectedness that I had felt in the mountains. Nothing ... *nothing*—not hard canoeing, hard portaging, helping my fellow voyagers, conversation, or hunger—diluted the peace I was experiencing. As in Montana, I felt content and happy beyond words. Apophatic. My entire being was in prayer, open to creation, and I felt directly connected to God.

Once again, there was no place on earth I would have rather been at that time. For the next six hours I was a canoeing, portaging, helping, hungry *prayer*, apophatic in a new, active way. I was more in touch with the awe-inspiring than I felt I had any right to be, and while the feeling gradually ebbed, the sense of grace did not.

Joseph Campbell, a noted professor of both comparative myth and comparative religion who spent a lifetime looking at the inner issues that drive people, once wrote:

> People say that what we are all seeking is meaning for life. I don't think that's what we're really seeking. I think that what we're seeking is an experience of being alive, so that our life experience on the purely physical plane will have resonance within our own innermost being and reality, so that we actually feel *the rapture of being alive*.[2] [italics added]

I believe Campbell was exactly right. I also believe that, in feeling the rapture of life, we find the meaning of it.

AMAZING GRACE

A mind that is stretched by a new experience can never go back to its old dimensions.
—*Oliver Wendell Holmes (1809–1894)*

On Renewal in the Wilderness trips people don't talk so much about how tired they are or how wobbly their legs are from hard portages or how scratched up they are, but they do talk about testing themselves and sensing a spiritual openness, even awe, as if scales are dropping from their souls. I'm fascinated with the words they use, wonderful contradictory words that show the richness of the experience: exhausted, energized; uplifting, frightening; exhilaration, trepidation. Many others say their experiences are beyond description. When we sit around a campfire with fellow travelers who've had their own nearly indescribable experiences, as we try to put words to them, there is much silent nodding of heads, perhaps a few quiet "amens." No other explanation is necessary because the experience is understood and shared—apophatic—usually beyond the capability of language.

> These adventures are a particular time and place. They can never be recreated, only remembered. They are best recalled quietly among participants with a wry and wistful smile and a nodding acknowledgment that even though we appear to be as we once were, inside we have been changed by the experience. To attempt to explain it more fully to people who were not there is futile.
>
> —Bryan C. Abbott, on a canoe trip
> on the Wisconsin River

The one thing we share—spoken or unspoken—is our acknowledgment of the astounding, quiet ability of the wilderness to change lives, which was expressed with heart by a woman who faced the trial of a hike down the Grand Canyon.

> I can't even fully capture in words what happened to me when I was out there. The first day when I looked out over the lip of the canyon and looked down, and saw the trail that we were headed down, knowing that my knees were weak to begin with ... and my spirit as well, I thought to myself, "there's no way I can do that." And yet, five days later, my body incredibly tired, I felt more alive than I had in all my life.
>
> But it's not just that I felt physically healthier ... and still do.... I feel more balanced and secure. It's like that was the spark I needed to feel competent and able to handle my life again. It sparked a flame inside me that I can't remember feeling since I was a young girl.... It's like the spirit is

burning deep inside me again, and I'm looking at my life a little differently.... I wouldn't give it up for anything.[3]

The Bible has a phrase about "seeing through a glass darkly" (1 Corinthians 13:12), which is an apt description of our clouded vision when we see life, in all its stupefying complexity, through eyes darkened by the distractions of modern living. A genuine immersion in a wilderness experience is one of the few ways I know to experience God so directly—to begin seeing through the glass clearly. In the wild places beyond our control, we can experience and reexperience God in tap-root deepness and clarity that is nearly impossible anywhere else.

Even atheists have experiences in the wilderness that transcend the normal boundaries of their lives and move them to believe that they've connected to the larger universe. They, too, have that Something Bigger than Us experience, that sense of smallness and insignificance amid the natural grandeur and immensity that is everywhere we look in the deep wilderness. And while they may not call those experiences "spiritual," they know they've been touched in ways that defy both reason and explanation. As one atheist put it, "If I want to get a sense of my own spirituality or sense of self ... I want to go somewhere where there's trees and water ... to connect with myself, and once I do that, then I am connected with something larger than myself."[4]

Wild places do have an amazing ability to clear the dark film through which we usually see. When we enter nature with a willingness to be surprised—and not confined to the boxes of expectations that we often build—and immerse ourselves in the silence and solitude the wilderness offers, the Sturm und Drang of "civilized" living comes into sharp contrast. Problems take on new and healthier perspective; amazing "heart" things happen.

I've discovered, in the wilderness, that our hearts are much wiser than our heads, especially when it comes to spiritual things. In ancient days, the heart was considered the center of all the operations of human life, including spiritual matters. This makes sense to me, because in the days when I had no use for God, my *mind* could talk me out of God in an instant. But my heart held greater wisdom.

In the wilderness, where things are silent and simple and unclouded by puny human strivings, the heart, unlike the mind—at least my mind—is willing to go way beyond the rational and into the spiritual, way past the limits of the possible into the limitlessness of Possibility. I like to think of it as LASIK surgery, but for the soul!

> *I anticipated an enjoyable adventure with a group of longtime friends, but found something more—a spiritual awakening, which I had given up hope of ever finding and which I did not anticipate ever finding.... This wilderness trip launched me into another set of surprising adventures, which have only deepened my resolve and hope. Through it, I finally began to realize and understand the meaning of Amazing Grace.*
>
> —Gordon M. Mallett, on a canoe trip
> on the Wisconsin River

In the wilderness, whole new worlds open up, frightening and exciting in equal parts, but life renewing, and so stretching that we can never go back to our old shape.

HOLY AGAIN

> Ask the animals, and they will teach you; the birds of the air, and they will tell you; ask the plants of the earth and they will teach you; and the fish of the sea will declare to you. Who among all these does not know that the hand of the Lord has done this? In his hand is the life of every living thing and the breath of every human being.
>
> —Job 12:7–10

One of my most enduring Alaska memories is of a day hike from one of our layover campsites deep in the Northern Talkeetnas. Unburdened by our heavy packs, we hiked up a steep mountain through a saddle pass to another mountain, then looked down on our campsite, our outpost of temporary civilization. We had to look hard to find it; our bright orange-yellow tents looked like microscopic kernels of unpopped corn, and were nearly invisible against the endless span of green and gray wilderness. The sense of our tininess in the immensity of Alaska was humbling in every way imaginable, and it made our group stop and quietly reflect, again, on how insignificant we are and how majestic God's universe is. Wyoming has a new advertising slogan, headlined on a photograph of beautiful alpine lake scenery, that says: "For generations, finding yourself has come right after discovering your insignificance." Wonderful! And true! Has the spiritual truth of finding ourselves through discovering our minusculeness gone mainstream? One can only hope, but it is a feeling that was expressed on the other side of the world three thousand years earlier in the eighth psalm:

> When I look at your heavens, the work of your fingers, the moon and the stars that you have established; what are human beings that you are mindful of them, mortals that you care for them? ... Our Sovereign, how majestic is your name in all the earth! (Psalm 8:3–4, 9)

Or, as one of our Renewal in the Wilderness participants wrote:

> *Being in the wilderness, there are no levels of abstraction that one has to work through to see God's work.... When you look at the stars and realize that you are looking at something that billions of others have viewed for thousands of years, you gain a better sense of the ages and your place there, and that this place is to be respected and passed on.*
>
> —Tom Leavens, on a canoe trip
> on the Wisconsin River

At a very visceral level, we humans crave the wild splendor of God, and we're powerfully drawn (at least visually) to nature's wild places. People who study these things have found that simply being in the wilderness creates a "joining" of extreme states of awareness (consciousness) and acuity, which lead to "peak" experiences that the recipient finds deeply spiritual. It's like several streams meeting at one point to form a mighty and untamed river.

Some, such as this woman who hiked in the Grand Canyon, describe this as an experience of transcendence:

> Stopping for a moment and looking up to see the full moon rising ... I felt a complete merging with the surrounding environment [as if] I was moving into it in some way ... or rather it was moving into me.... I suppose what I experienced was transcendence.... It was expansive and at first I was afraid and then deeply comforted and filled with a sense of complete peace.[5]

Others have put it more simply, describing it as being "holy again":

> Being in such a pristine, remote area lets me step back from my life and put it into perspective, to re-focus on the things that really matter. It's something about being put back in touch with the essential.... Out there in the wilderness I am able to see my life as simple and holy again.[6]

Or, as a simple Navajo prayer reminds us, "I am restored in beauty. I am restored in beauty. I am restored in beauty."

Every time we accept the challenge of the wilderness, we remember what flows in our veins: a spirit of adventure that even the practical requirements and necessary barnacles of daily living cannot completely bury. Every time we see the glory of a desert flower it reminds us that we are, deep down, filled with grace. Every time we paddle a canoe or navigate a rapids, it brings soul-popping moisture to our often dry, weighted lives.

Make no mistake, however. If you choose to follow your heart and prevail over your misgivings about being in the wilderness, if you respond to the "call of the wild," the wilderness will take you away from your comfort zone; it will test you in many ways. All of them good. All of them worth it. You'll feel your body again. You'll learn what things you really need. And you will be astonished at how little you need to be profoundly happy.

You'll also be newly aware of how frequently and how thoroughly you may have put both God and yourself into boxes of expectations that simply do not apply, and that limit you both. At a gut level, you'll come to understand how freeing it is to trade your expectations for Possibilities, to trade your fears for Hopes, to trade your dark, filmy view for Clarity.

In the wilderness you'll be put on edges that will allow the life-renewing things to happen. You'll find that being constantly in the present, as the wilderness demands, is the time in which these things do happen, and that silence and solitude are wonderful gifts. You'll learn to see the Divine in the small things of life, as well as in the astonishing grandeur that is often beyond words.

In other words, you'll reconnect with the physical world, and in that connection you stand a good chance of experiencing the transcendent—especially if you're open to the surprises.

As one surprised pilgrim described it:

A spiritual experience junkie I am not ... but as I stood at the edge and gazed upon the spectacular view below me ... alone, in the silence and sparseness of the desert ... I knew I was in a spiritual encounter once again.... The feeling was overpowering and wonderful.

> —Gary Benz, at the rotunda of Herod's palace
> in the ancient Jewish citadel of Masada

As you consider what you want for your life, perhaps the best question is the bedrock challenge of the American poet Mary Oliver, "What is it you plan to do with your one wild and precious life?"[7] This is the question that has haunted humans since we rose above subsistence levels; it may be *the* question that we avoid by drowning ourselves with busyness so we don't have to confront it; and it's the question that calls us to seek answers beyond our confined boxes, for the reply often lies outside.

To borrow from the master bard, Shakespeare, "Get thee away!" Get thee to the wilderness! Go to nature to lose and to find yourself. Go to the edge to reclaim and redefine yourself. Go beyond old boundaries to see new horizons. And in the doing and *being* of your wildly courageous act, you'll experience what is offered to us all with great abundance: renewal in the wilderness.

NOTES

CHAPTER 2: IT'S IN OUR DNA

1. Matthew 4:1–11, Mark 1:12–13, Luke 4:1–4.
2. Camille and Kabir Helminski, trans., *Rumi—Daylight: A Daybook of Spiritual Guidance* (Putney, VT: Threshold Books, 1994), 67.
3. Han-shan, quoted in Stephen Mitchell, trans., *The Enlightened Heart: An Anthology of Sacred Poetry* (New York: Harper Perennial, 1993).
4. Joseph Epes Brown, ed., *The Sacred Pipe: Black Elk's Account of the Seven Rites of the Ogala Sioux* (Baltimore: Penguin Books, 1972).
5. *National Geographic Adventure* (March/April 2001).
6. Richard Louv, *Last Child in the Woods: Saving Our Children from Nature-Deficit Disorder* (Chapel Hill, NC: Algonquin Books, 2005).
7. Benedicta Ward, trans., *The Sayings of the Desert Fathers* (Kalamazoo: Cistercian Publications, 1984), 217.
8. Laura M. Fredrickson and Dorothy H. Anderson, "A Qualitative Exploration of the Wilderness Experience as a Source of Spiritual Inspiration," *Journal of Environmental Psychology* 19 (1999): 31.

CHAPTER 3: PRESENCE IN THE PRESENT

1. John Calvin, *Institutes of the Christian Religion*, I.5.1, I.6.6: 51–52, 69–70.
2. Blair Bertrand and Peter T. Hazelrigg, "Wandering Through the Wilderness: The Relationship Between Old Testament Wilderness Narratives and Contemporary Christian Camp Ministry" (unpublished paper, Princeton Theological Seminary, December 2, 2002): 28, 29.

3. Ibid., 28, 29.

4. Fredrickson and Anderson, "A Qualitative Exploration," 22.

CHAPTER 4: SCRAPING THE HULL

1. David Rensberger, "Deserted Places," *Weavings: A Journal of the Christian Spiritual Life: The Desert* 16, no. 3 (May/June, 2001): 9.

2. Fredrickson and Anderson, "A Qualitative Exploration," 30–31.

3. Elizabeth Canham, *A Table of Delight: Feasting with God in the Wilderness* (Nashville: Upper Rooms Books, 2005), 6.

4. Edward Edinger, *Ego and Archetype: Individuation and the Religious Function of the Psyche* (Boston: Shambhala, 1992), 50.

5. Andrew Louth, *The Wilderness of God* (Nashville: Abingdon Press, 1991), 42.

CHAPTER 5: GOD IN A BOX

1. Denise Linn, *Quest: A Guide for Creating Your Own Vision Quest* (New York: Ballantine, 1997), 5.

2. Adapted from Idries Shah, ed., *Tales of the Dervishes* (New York: Dutton, 1969), 23–24.

3. T. Carmi, ed. and trans., *The Penguin Book of Hebrew Verse* (New York: Viking Press, 1981), 338.

4. Ralph Waldo Emerson, *Nature* (Boston: Beacon Press, 1985).

CHAPTER 6: GOD ON THE EDGE

1. Joseph Epes Brown, *The Spiritual Legacy of the American Indian* (New York: Crossroad, 1998).

2. J. N. Figgis quoted in *Outward Bound Readings* (Concord, MA: n.d.), 26.

3. Belden Lane, *The Solace of Fierce Landscapes: Exploring Desert and Mountain Spirituality* (New York: Oxford University Press, 1998), 19.

4. Helminski, *Rumi—Daylight*, 23.

5. Lane, *The Solace of Fierce Landscapes*, 46.

6. Fredrickson and Anderson, "A Qualitative Exploration," 33.

7. W. Scott Olsen, "An Advent Nature," in *The Sacred Place: Witnessing the Holy in the Physical World*, ed. W. Scott Olsen and Scott Cairns (Salt Lake City: University of Utah Press, 1966), 335.

CHAPTER 7: HEALING WATERS

1. Igjugarjuk quoted in *National Geographic Adventure* (March/April 2001).

2. Thompson Gale, ed., *Encyclopedia of Religion*, 2nd ed. (New York: MacMillan Reference, 2005), 2301.

3. David Douglas, "Inviting Solitude: Notes in the Desert Silence," *Weavings: A Journal of the Christian Spiritual Life* 16, no. 3 (May/June 2001): 16.

4. Rensberger, "Deserted Places," 9.

5. Calvin, *Institutes of the Christian Religion*, I.5.1, I.6.6: 51–52, 69–70.

6. Fredrickson and Anderson, "A Qualitative Exploration," 31.

7. Lane, *Solace of Fierce Landscapes*, 67.

8. Tom Shealey, "The Gift of Quiet," *Backpacker* (February 2002): 9–10.

9. Frederickson and Anderson, "A Qualitative Exploration," 32.

10. Ibid.

11. Ibid.

12. Ibid., 31.

CHAPTER 8: THE RAPTURE OF BEING ALIVE

1. Kathryn Williams and David Harvey, "Transcendent Experience in Forest Environments," *Journal of Environmental Psychology* (2001): 255.

2. Joseph Campbell, with Bill Moyers, *The Power of Myth* (New York: Doubleday, 1988), 5.

3. Fredrickson and Anderson, "A Qualitative Exploration," 33.

4. Ibid., 34.

5. Ibid.

6. Ibid.

7. Mary Oliver, "The Summer Day," *New and Selected Poems* (Boston: Beacon Press, 1992), 94.

SUGGESTIONS FOR FURTHER READING

BOOKS

Campbell, Joseph, with Bill Moyers. *The Power of Myth*. New York: Doubleday, 1988.

Canham, Elizabeth. *A Table of Delight: Feasting with God in the Wilderness*. Nashville: Upper Room Books, 2005.

Comins, Mike. *A Wild Faith: Jewish Ways into Wildness, Wilderness Ways into Judaism*. Woodstck, VT: Jewish Lights Publishing, 2007.

Easwaran, Eknath. *God Makes the Rivers to Flow: Sacred Literature of the World*. Tomales, CA: Nilgiri Press, 2003.

Feiler, Bruce. *Abraham: A Journey to the Hearts of Three Faiths*. New York: W. Morrow, 2002.

———. *Walking the Bible: A Journey by Land through the Five Books of Moses*. New York: W. Morrow, 2001.

Harden, Philip. *Journeys of Simplicity: Traveling Light with Thomas Merton, Bashō, Edward Abbey, Annie Dillard & Others*. Woodstock, VT: SkyLight Paths Publishing, 2003.

Highland, Chris, ed. *Meditations of John Muir: Nature's Temple*. Berkeley, CA: Wilderness Press, 2005.

Kent, Rockwell. *Wilderness: A Journal of Quiet Adventure in Alaska*. Hanover, NH: University Press of New England, 1996.

Lane, Belden. *The Solace of Fierce Landscapes: Exploring Desert and Mountain Spirituality*. New York: Oxford University Press, 1998.

Louth, Andrew. *The Wilderness of God*. Nashville: Abingdon Press, 1991.

Rohr, Richard. *Everything Belongs: The Gift of Contemplative Prayer.* New York: Crossroad, 2003.

Tolle, Eckhart. *The Power of Now: A Guide to Spiritual Enlightenment.* Novato, CA: New World Library, 1999.

MAGAZINES

Backpacker: The Outdoors at Your Doorstep. Emmaus, NJ.

About Renewal
in the Wilderness

Renewal in the Wilderness takes men and women—generally in their middle years—away from their normal "civilized" environments for one to eight days of wilderness travel to have a very good time, and to spend time with God. Seeking a closer relationship with God in wild places is an impulse that is both eons old and global, and we tap into this ancient and proven connection when we trade our everyday comforts for the silence and solitude of nature. It is as effective today as it than four thousand years ago.

Six hundred years ago John Calvin said that nature is God's cathedral, and that's what we find today as well. Our time in "God's cathedral" is intentionally designed to provide a spiritual environment in which people can renew, or explore, their relationships with God in places that are so obviously of God's making. Our participants have been from many faith traditions and, often enough, from none.

All our trips to date have been by canoe or kayak, so participants need not be in great shape to go as deeply into the wilderness as time will allow. Join us: Surprise yourself and thrill God.

For specific trip dates and details, you can reach us at:

E-mail: renewalitw@joltmail.com
www.renewalinthewilderness.org

Global Spiritual Perspectives

Spiritual Perspectives on America's Role as Superpower
by the Editors at SkyLight Paths
Are we the world's good neighbor or a global bully? From a spiritual perspective, what are America's responsibilities as the only remaining superpower? Contributors:
Dr. Beatrice Bruteau • Dr. Joan Brown Campbell • Tony Campolo • Rev. Forrest Church • Lama Surya Das • Matthew Fox • Kabir Helminski • Thich Nhat Hanh • Eboo Patel • Abbot M. Basil Pennington, ocso • Dennis Prager • Rosemary Radford Ruether • Wayne Teasdale • Rev. William McD. Tully • Rabbi Arthur Waskow • John Wilson
5½ x 8½, 256 pp, Quality PB, 978-1-893361-81-2 **$16.95**

Spiritual Perspectives on Globalization, 2nd Edition
Making Sense of Economic and Cultural Upheaval
by Ira Rifkin; Foreword by Dr. David Little, Harvard Divinity School
What is globalization? Surveys the religious landscape. Includes a new Discussion Guide designed for group use.
5½ x 8½, 256 pp, Quality PB, 978-1-59473-045-0 **$16.99**

Hinduism / Vedanta

The Four Yogas
A Guide to the Spiritual Paths of Action, Devotion, Meditation and Knowledge
by Swami Adiswarananda 6 x 9, 320 pp, HC, 978-1-59473-143-3 **$29.99**

Meditation & Its Practices
A Definitive Guide to Techniques and Traditions of Meditation in Yoga and Vedanta
by Swami Adiswarananda 6 x 9, 504 pp, Quality PB, 978-1-59473-105-1 **$19.99**

The Spiritual Quest and the Way of Yoga: The Goal, the Journey and the Milestones
by Swami Adiswarananda 6 x 9, 288 pp, HC, 978-1-59473-113-6 **$29.99**

Sri Ramakrishna, the Face of Silence
by Swami Nikhilananda and Dhan Gopal Mukerji
Edited with an Introduction by Swami Adiswarananda; Foreword by Dhan Gopal Mukerji II
Classic biographies present the life and thought of Sri Ramakrishna.
6 x 9, 352 pp, HC, 978-1-59473-115-0 **$29.99**

Sri Sarada Devi, The Holy Mother
Her Teachings and Conversations
Translated with Notes by Swami Nikhilananda; Edited with an Introduction by Swami Adiswarananda
6 x 9, 288 pp, HC, 978-1-59473-070-2 **$29.99**

The Vedanta Way to Peace and Happiness *by Swami Adiswarananda*
6 x 9, 240 pp, HC, 978-1-59473-034-4 **$29.99**

Vivekananda, World Teacher: His Teachings on the Spiritual Unity of Humankind
Edited and with an Introduction by Swami Adiswarananda
6 x 9, 272 pp, Quality PB, 978-1-59473-210-2 **$21.99**

Sikhism

The First Sikh Spiritual Master
Timeless Wisdom from the Life and Teachings of Guru Nanak *by Harish Dhillon*
Tells the story of a unique spiritual leader who showed a gentle, peaceful path to God-realization while highlighting Guru Nanak's quest for tolerance and compassion. 6 x 9, 192 pp, Quality PB, 978-1-59473-209-6 **$16.99**

Or phone, fax, mail or e-mail to: SKYLIGHT PATHS Publishing
Sunset Farm Offices, Route 4 • P.O. Box 237 • Woodstock, Vermont 05091
Tel: (802) 457-4000 • Fax: (802) 457-4004 • www.skylightpaths.com
Credit card orders: (800) 962-4544 (8:30AM–5:30PM ET Monday–Friday)
Generous discounts on quantity orders. SATISFACTION GUARANTEED. Prices subject to change.

Spirituality

Jewish Spirituality: A Brief Introduction for Christians   *by Lawrence Kushner*
5½ x 8½, 112 pp, Quality PB, 978-1-58023-150-3 **$12.95** *(a Jewish Lights book)*

Journeys of Simplicity: Traveling Light with Thomas Merton, Bashō, Edward Abbey, Annie Dillard & Others   *by Philip Harnden* 5 x 7¼, 128 pp, HC, 978-1-893361-76-8 **$16.95**

Keeping Spiritual Balance As We Grow Older: More than 65 Creative Ways to Use Purpose, Prayer, and the Power of Spirit to Build a Meaningful Retirement   *by Molly and Bernie Srode* 8 x 8, 224 pp, Quality PB, 978-1-59473-042-9 **$16.99**

The Monks of Mount Athos: A Western Monk's Extraordinary Spiritual Journey on Eastern Holy Ground   *by M. Basil Pennington, ocso; Foreword by Archimandrite Dionysios* 6 x 9, 256 pp, 10+ b/w line drawings, Quality PB, 978-1-893361-78-2 **$18.95**

One God Clapping: The Spiritual Path of a Zen Rabbi   *by Alan Lew with Sherrill Jaffe* 5½ x 8½, 336 pp, Quality PB, 978-1-58023-115-2 **$16.95** *(a Jewish Lights book)*

Prayer for People Who Think Too Much: A Guide to Everyday, Anywhere Prayer from the World's Faith Traditions   *by Mitch Finley* 5½ x 8½, 224 pp, Quality PB, 978-1-893361-21-8 **$16.99**; HC, 978-1-893361-00-3 **$21.95**

Show Me Your Way: The Complete Guide to Exploring Interfaith Spiritual Direction   *by Howard A. Addison* 5½ x 8½, 240 pp, Quality PB, 978-1-893361-41-6 **$16.95**

Spirituality 101: The Indispensable Guide to Keeping—or Finding—Your Spiritual Life on Campus   *by Harriet L. Schwartz, with contributions from college students at nearly thirty campuses across the United States* 6 x 9, 272 pp, Quality PB, 978-1-59473-000-9 **$16.99**

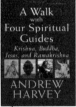

Spiritually Incorrect: Finding God in All the Wrong Places   *by Dan Wakefield; Illus. by Marian DelVecchio* 5½ x 8½, 192 pp, b/w illus., Quality PB, 978-1-59473-137-2 **$15.99**

Spiritual Manifestos: Visions for Renewed Religious Life in America from Young Spiritual Leaders of Many Faiths   *Edited by Niles Elliot Goldstein; Preface by Martin E. Marty* 6 x 9, 256 pp, HC, 978-1-893361-09-6 **$21.95**

A Walk with Four Spiritual Guides: Krishna, Buddha, Jesus, and Ramakrishna   *by Andrew Harvey* 5½ x 8½, 192 pp, 10 b/w photos & illus., Quality PB, 978-1-59473-138-9 **$15.99**

What Matters: Spiritual Nourishment for Head and Heart   *by Frederick Franck* 5 x 7¼, 128 pp, 50+ b/w illus., HC, 978-1-59473-013-9 **$16.99**

Who Is My God?, 2nd Edition: An Innovative Guide to Finding Your Spiritual Identity   *Created by the Editors at SkyLight Paths* 6 x 9, 160 pp, Quality PB, 978-1-59473-014-6 **$15.99**

Spirituality—A Week Inside

Come and Sit: A Week Inside Meditation Centers
by Marcia Z. Nelson; Foreword by Wayne Teasdale
The insider's guide to meditation in a variety of different spiritual traditions— Buddhist, Hindu, Christian, Jewish, and Sufi traditions.
6 x 9, 224 pp, b/w photos, Quality PB, 978-1-893361-35-5 **$16.95**

Lighting the Lamp of Wisdom: A Week Inside a Yoga Ashram
by John Ittner; Foreword by Dr. David Frawley
This insider's guide to Hindu spiritual life takes you into a typical week of retreat inside a yoga ashram to demystify the experience and show you what to expect.
6 x 9, 192 pp, 10+ b/w photos, Quality PB, 978-1-893361-52-2 **$15.95**

Making a Heart for God: A Week Inside a Catholic Monastery
by Dianne Aprile; Foreword by Brother Patrick Hart, ocso
Takes you to the Abbey of Gethsemani—the Trappist monastery in Kentucky that was home to author Thomas Merton—to explore the details.
6 x 9, 224 pp, b/w photos, Quality PB, 978-1-893361-49-2 **$16.95**

Waking Up: A Week Inside a Zen Monastery
by Jack Maguire; Foreword by John Daido Loori, Roshi
An essential guide to what it's like to spend a week inside a Zen Buddhist monastery.
6 x 9, 224 pp, b/w photos, Quality PB, 978-1-893361-55-3 **$16.95**
HC, 978-1-893361-13-3 **$21.95**

Spiritual Biography—SkyLight Lives

SkyLight Lives reintroduces the lives and works of key spiritual figures of our time—people who by their teaching or example have challenged our assumptions about spirituality and have caused us to look at it in new ways.

 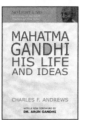  

The Life of Evelyn Underhill
An Intimate Portrait of the Groundbreaking Author of *Mysticism*
by Margaret Cropper; Foreword by Dana Greene
Evelyn Underhill was a passionate writer and teacher who wrote elegantly on mysticism, worship, and devotional life.
6 x 9, 288 pp, 5 b/w photos, Quality PB, 978-1-893361-70-6 **$18.95**

Mahatma Gandhi: His Life and Ideas
by Charles F. Andrews; Foreword by Dr. Arun Gandhi
Examines from a contemporary Christian activist's point of view the religious ideas and political dynamics that influenced the birth of the peaceful resistance movement.
6 x 9, 336 pp, 5 b/w photos, Quality PB, 978-1-893361-89-8 **$18.95**

Simone Weil: A Modern Pilgrimage
by Robert Coles
The extraordinary life of the spiritual philosopher who's been called both saint and madwoman.
6 x 9, 208 pp, Quality PB, 978-1-893361-34-8 **$16.95**

Zen Effects: The Life of Alan Watts
by Monica Furlong
Through his widely popular books and lectures, Alan Watts (1915–1973) did more to introduce Eastern philosophy and religion to Western minds than any figure before or since.
6 x 9, 264 pp, Quality PB, 978-1-893361-32-4 **$16.95**

More Spiritual Biography

Bede Griffiths: An Introduction to His Interspiritual Thought
by Wayne Teasdale
The first study of his contemplative experience and thought, exploring the intersection of Hinduism and Christianity.
6 x 9, 288 pp, Quality PB, 978-1-893361-77-5 **$18.95**

The Soul of the Story: Meetings with Remarkable People
by Rabbi David Zeller
Inspiring and entertaining, this compelling collection of spiritual adventures assures us that no spiritual lesson truly learned is ever lost.
6 x 9, 288 pp, HC, 978-1-58023-272-2 **$21.99** *(a Jewish Lights book)*

Spiritual Poetry—The Mystic Poets

Experience these mystic poets as you never have before. Each beautiful, compact book includes: a brief introduction to the poet's time and place; a summary of the major themes of the poet's mysticism and religious tradition; essential selections from the poet's most important works; and an appreciative preface by a contemporary spiritual writer.

Hafiz: The Mystic Poets
Preface by Ibrahim Gamard
Hafiz is known throughout the world as Persia's greatest poet, with sales of his poems in Iran today only surpassed by those of the Qur'an itself. His probing and joyful verse speaks to people from all backgrounds who long to taste and feel divine love and experience harmony with all living things.
5 x 7¼, 144 pp, HC, 978-1-59473-009-2 **$16.99**

Hopkins: The Mystic Poets
Preface by Rev. Thomas Ryan, CSP
Gerard Manley Hopkins, Christian mystical poet, is beloved for his use of fresh language and startling metaphors to describe the world around him. Although his verse is lovely, beneath the surface lies a searching soul, wrestling with and yearning for God.
5 x 7¼, 112 pp, HC, 978-1-59473-010-8 **$16.99**

Tagore: The Mystic Poets
Preface by Swami Adiswarananda
Rabindranath Tagore is often considered the "Shakespeare" of modern India. A great mystic, Tagore was the teacher of W. B. Yeats and Robert Frost, the close friend of Albert Einstein and Mahatma Gandhi, and the winner of the Nobel Prize for Literature. This beautiful sampling of Tagore's two most important works, *The Gardener* and *Gitanjali,* offers a glimpse into his spiritual vision that has inspired people around the world.
5 x 7¼, 144 pp, HC, 978-1-59473-008-5 **$16.99**

Whitman: The Mystic Poets
Preface by Gary David Comstock
Walt Whitman was the most innovative and influential poet of the nineteenth century. This beautiful sampling of Whitman's most important poetry from *Leaves of Grass,* and selections from his prose writings, offers a glimpse into the spiritual side of his most radical themes—love for country, love for others, and love of Self.
5 x 7¼, 192 pp, HC, 978-1-59473-041-2 **$16.99**

Meditation / Prayer

Prayers to an Evolutionary God
by William Cleary; Afterword by Diarmuid O'Murchu

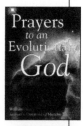

How is it possible to pray when God is dislocated from heaven, dispersed all around us, and more of a creative force than an all-knowing father? Inspired by the spiritual and scientific teachings of Diarmuid O'Murchu and Teilhard de Chardin, Cleary reveals that religion and science can be combined to create an expanding view of the universe—an evolutionary faith.
6 x 9, 208 pp, HC, 978-1-59473-006-1 **$21.99**

Psalms: A Spiritual Commentary
by M. Basil Pennington, OCSO; Illustrations by Phillip Ratner

Showing how the Psalms give profound and candid expression to both our highest aspirations and our deepest pain, the late, highly respected Cistercian Abbot M. Basil Pennington shares his reflections on some of the most beloved passages from the Bible's most widely read book.
6 x 9, 176 pp, HC, 24 full-page b/w illus., 978-1-59473-141-9 **$19.99**

The Song of Songs: A Spiritual Commentary
by M. Basil Pennington, OCSO; Illustrations by Phillip Ratner
Join the late M. Basil Pennington as he ruminates on the Bible's most challenging mystical text. Follow a path into the Songs that weaves through his inspired words and the evocative drawings of Jewish artist Phillip Ratner—a path that reveals your own humanity and leads to the deepest delight of your soul.
6 x 9, 160 pp, HC, 14 b/w illus., 978-1-59473-004-7 **$19.99**

Women of Color Pray: Voices of Strength, Faith, Healing,
Hope and Courage   *Edited and with Introductions by Christal M. Jackson*
Through these prayers, poetry, lyrics, meditations and affirmations, you will share in the strong and undeniable connection women of color share with God. It will challenge you to explore new ways of prayerful expression.
5 x 7¼, 208 pp, Quality PB, 978-1-59473-077-1 **$15.99**

The Art of Public Prayer: Not for Clergy Only
by Lawrence A. Hoffman
An ecumenical resource for all people looking to change hardened worship patterns.
6 x 9, 288 pp, Quality PB, 978-1-893361-06-5 **$19.99**

Finding Grace at the Center, 3rd Ed.: The Beginning of Centering Prayer
by M. Basil Pennington, OCSO, Thomas Keating, OCSO, and Thomas E. Clarke, SJ
Foreword by Rev. Cynthia Bourgeault, PhD
5 x 7¼, 128 pp, Quality PB, 978-1-59473-182-2 **$12.99**

A Heart of Stillness: A Complete Guide to Learning the Art of Meditation
by David A. Cooper 5½ x 8½, 272 pp, Quality PB, 978-1-893361-03-4 **$16.95**

Meditation without Gurus: A Guide to the Heart of Practice
by Clark Strand 5½ x 8½, 192 pp, Quality PB, 978-1-893361-93-5 **$16.95**

Praying with Our Hands: 21 Practices of Embodied Prayer from the World's
Spiritual Traditions *by Jon M. Sweeney; Photographs by Jennifer J. Wilson; Foreword by Mother Tessa Bielecki; Afterword by Taitetsu Unno, PhD*
8 x 8, 96 pp, 22 duotone photos, Quality PB, 978-1-893361-16-4 **$16.95**

Silence, Simplicity & Solitude: A Complete Guide to Spiritual Retreat at Home
by David A. Cooper 5½ x 8½, 336 pp, Quality PB, 978-1-893361-04-1 **$16.95**

Three Gates to
Meditation Practice
A Personal Journey into
Sufism, Buddhism, and Judaism

David A. Cooper

Three Gates to Meditation Practice: A Personal Journey into Sufism, Buddhism,
and Judaism *by David A. Cooper* 5½ x 8½, 240 pp, Quality PB, 978-1-893361-22-5 **$16.95**

Women Pray: Voices through the Ages, from Many Faiths, Cultures and Traditions
Edited and with Introductions by Monica Furlong
5 x 7¼, 256 pp, Quality PB, 978-1-59473-071-9 **$15.99**
Deluxe HC with ribbon marker, 978-1-893361-25-6 **$19.95**

Sacred Texts—SkyLight Illuminations Series

Offers today's spiritual seeker an accessible entry into the great classic texts of the world's spiritual traditions. Each classic is presented in an accessible translation, with facing pages of guided commentary from experts, giving you the keys you need to understand the history, context and meaning of the text. This series enables you, whatever your background, to experience and understand classic spiritual texts directly, and to make them a part of your life.

CHRISTIANITY

The End of Days: Essential Selections from Apocalyptic Texts— Annotated & Explained *Annotation by Robert G. Clouse*
Helps you understand the complex Christian visions of the end of the world.
5½ x 8½, 224 pp, Quality PB, 978-1-59473-170-9 **$16.99**

The Hidden Gospel of Matthew: Annotated & Explained
Translation & Annotation by Ron Miller
Takes you deep into the text cherished around the world to discover the words and events that have the strongest connection to the historical Jesus.
5½ x 8½, 272 pp, Quality PB, 978-1-59473-038-2 **$16.99**

The Lost Sayings of Jesus: Teachings from Ancient Christian, Jewish, Gnostic and Islamic Sources—Annotated & Explained
Translation & Annotation by Andrew Phillip Smith; Foreword by Stephan A. Hoeller
This collection of more than three hundred sayings depicts Jesus as a Wisdom teacher who speaks to people of all faiths as a mystic and spiritual master.
5½ x 8½, 240 pp, Quality PB, 978-1-59473-172-3 **$16.99**

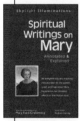

Philokalia: The Eastern Christian Spiritual Texts—Selections Annotated & Explained *Annotation by Allyne Smith; Translation by G. E. H. Palmer, Phillip Sherrard and Bishop Kallistos Ware*
The first approachable introduction to the wisdom of the Philokalia, which is the classic text of Eastern Christian spirituality.
5½ x 8½, 240 pp, Quality PB, 978-1-59473-103-7 **$16.99**

Spiritual Writings on Mary: Annotated & Explained
Annotation by Mary Ford-Grabowsky; Foreword by Andrew Harvey
Examines the role of Mary, the mother of Jesus, as a source of inspiration in history and in life today. 5½ x 8½, 288 pp, Quality PB, 978-1-59473-001-6 **$16.99**

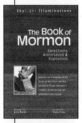

The Way of a Pilgrim: Annotated & Explained
Translation & Annotation by Gleb Pokrovsky; Foreword by Andrew Harvey
This classic of Russian spirituality is the delightful account of one man who sets out to learn the prayer of the heart, also known as the "Jesus prayer."
5½ x 8½, 160 pp, Illus., Quality PB, 978-1-893361-31-7 **$14.95**

MORMONISM

The Book of Mormon: Selections Annotated & Explained
Annotation by Jana Riess; Foreword by Phyllis Tickle
Explores the sacred epic that is cherished by more than twelve million members of the LDS church as the keystone of their faith.
5½ x 8½ , 272 pp, Quality PB, 978-1-59473-076-4 **$16.99**

NATIVE AMERICAN

Native American Stories of the Sacred: Annotated & Explained
Retold & Annotated by Evan T. Pritchard
Intended for more than entertainment, these teaching tales contain elegantly simple illustrations of time-honored truths.
5½ x 8½, 272 pp, Quality PB, 978-1-59473-112-9 **$16.99**

Sacred Texts—cont.

GNOSTICISM

The Gospel of Philip: Annotated & Explained
Translation & Annotation by Andrew Phillip Smith; Foreword by Stevan Davies
Reveals otherwise unrecorded sayings of Jesus and fragments of Gnostic mythology.
5½ x 8½, 160 pp, Quality PB, 978-1-59473-111-2 **$16.99**

The Gospel of Thomas: Annotated & Explained
Translation & Annotation by Stevan Davies Sheds new light on the origins of Christianity and
portrays Jesus as a wisdom-loving sage. 5½ x 8½, 192 pp, Quality PB, 978-1-893361-45-4 **$16.99**

The Secret Book of John: The Gnostic Gospel—Annotated & Explained
Translation & Annotation by Stevan Davies The most significant and influential text of
the ancient Gnostic religion. 5½ x 8½, 208 pp, Quality PB, 978-1-59473-082-5 **$16.99**

JUDAISM

The Divine Feminine in Biblical Wisdom Literature
Selections Annotated & Explained
Translation & Annotation by Rabbi Rami Shapiro; Foreword by Rev. Cynthia Bourgeault, PhD
Uses the Hebrew books of Psalms, Proverbs, Song of Songs, Ecclesiastes and Job,
Wisdom literature and the Wisdom of Solomon to clarify who Wisdom is.
5½ x 8½, 240 pp, Quality PB, 978-1-59473-109-9 **$16.99**

Ethics of the Sages: *Pirke Avot*—Annotated & Explained
Translation & Annotation by Rabbi Rami Shapiro Clarifies the ethical teachings of the
early Rabbis. 5½ x 8½, 192 pp, Quality PB, 978-1-59473-207-2 **$16.99**

Hasidic Tales: Annotated & Explained
Translation & Annotation by Rabbi Rami Shapiro
Introduces the legendary tales of the impassioned Hasidic rabbis, presenting them as
stories rather than as parables. 5½ x 8½, 240 pp, Quality PB, 978-1-893361-86-7 **$16.95**

The Hebrew Prophets: Selections Annotated & Explained
Translation & Annotation by Rabbi Rami Shapiro; Foreword by Zalman M. Schachter-Shalomi
Focuses on the central themes covered by all the Hebrew prophets.
5½ x 8½, 224 pp, Quality PB, 978-1-59473-037-5 **$16.99**

Zohar: Annotated & Explained   *Translation & Annotation by Daniel C. Matt*
The best-selling author of *The Essential Kabbalah* brings together in one place the most
important teachings of the Zohar, the canonical text of Jewish mystical tradition.
5½ x 8½, 176 pp, Quality PB, 978-1-893361-51-5 **$15.99**

EASTERN RELIGIONS

Bhagavad Gita: Annotated & Explained   *Translation by Shri Purohit Swami*
Annotation by Kendra Crossen Burroughs Explains references and philosophical terms,
shares the interpretations of famous spiritual leaders and scholars, and more.
5½ x 8½, 192 pp, Quality PB, 978-1-893361-28-7 **$16.95**

Dhammapada: Annotated & Explained   *Translation by Max Müller and revised by*
Jack Maguire; Annotation by Jack Maguire Contains all of Buddhism's key teachings.
5½ x 8½, 160 pp, b/w photos, Quality PB, 978-1-893361-42-3 **$14.95**

Rumi and Islam: Selections from His Stories, Poems, and Discourses—
Annotated & Explained   *Translation & Annotation by Ibrahim Gamard*
Focuses on Rumi's place within the Sufi tradition of Islam, providing insight into
the mystical side of the religion. 5½ x 8½, 240 pp, Quality PB, 978-1-59473-002-3 **$15.99**

Selections from the Gospel of Sri Ramakrishna: Annotated & Explained
Translation by Swami Nikhilananda; Annotation by Kendra Crossen Burroughs
Introduces the fascinating world of the Indian mystic and the universal appeal
of his message. 5½ x 8½, 240 pp, b/w photos, Quality PB, 978-1-893361-46-1 **$16.95**

Tao Te Ching: Annotated & Explained   *Translation & Annotation by Derek Lin*
Foreword by Lama Surya Das Introduces an Eastern classic in an accessible, poetic
and completely original way. 5½ x 8½, 192 pp, Quality PB, 978-1-59473-204-1 **$16.99**

Spirituality of the Seasons

Autumn: A Spiritual Biography of the Season
Edited by Gary Schmidt and Susan M. Felch; Illustrations by Mary Azarian
Rejoice in autumn as a time of preparation and reflection. Includes Wendell Berry, David James Duncan, Robert Frost, A. Bartlett Giamatti, E. B. White, P. D. James, Julian of Norwich, Garret Keizer, Tracy Kidder, Anne Lamott, May Sarton.
6 x 9, 320 pp, 5 b/w illus., Quality PB, 978-1-59473-118-1 **$18.99**
HC, 978-1-59473-005-4 **$22.99**

Spring: A Spiritual Biography of the Season
Edited by Gary Schmidt and Susan M. Felch; Illustrations by Mary Azarian

Explore the gentle unfurling of spring and reflect on how nature celebrates rebirth and renewal. Includes Jane Kenyon, Lucy Larcom, Harry Thurston, Nathaniel Hawthorne, Noel Perrin, Annie Dillard, Martha Ballard, Barbara Kingsolver, Dorothy Wordsworth, Donald Hall, David Brill, Lionel Basney, Isak Dinesen, Paul Laurence Dunbar. 6 x 9, 352 pp, 6 b/w illus., HC, 978-1-59473-114-3 **$21.99**

Summer: A Spiritual Biography of the Season
Edited by Gary Schmidt and Susan M. Felch; Illustrations by Barry Moser
"A sumptuous banquet.... These selections lift up an exquisite wholeness found within an everyday sophistication."— ★ *Publishers Weekly* starred review
Includes Anne Lamott, Luci Shaw, Ray Bradbury, Richard Selzer, Thomas Lynch, Walt Whitman, Carl Sandburg, Sherman Alexie, Madeleine L'Engle, Jamaica Kincaid.
6 x 9, 304 pp, 5 b/w illus., Quality PB, 978-1-59473-183-9 **$18.99**
HC, 978-1-59473-083-2 **$21.99**

Winter: A Spiritual Biography of the Season
Edited by Gary Schmidt and Susan M. Felch; Illustrations by Barry Moser
"This outstanding anthology features top-flight nature and spirituality writers on the fierce, inexorable season of winter.... Remarkably lively and warm, despite the icy subject." — ★ *Publishers Weekly* starred review.
Includes Will Campbell, Rachel Carson, Annie Dillard, Donald Hall, Ron Hansen, Jane Kenyon, Jamaica Kincaid, Barry Lopez, Kathleen Norris, John Updike, E. B. White.
6 x 9, 288 pp, 6 b/w illus., Deluxe PB w/flaps, 978-1-893361-92-8 **$18.95**
HC, 978-1-893361-53-9 **$21.95**

Spirituality / Animal Companions

Blessing the Animals: Prayers and Ceremonies to Celebrate God's Creatures, Wild and Tame *Edited by Lynn L. Caruso* 5 x 7¼, 256 pp, HC, 978-1-59473-145-7 **$19.99**

What Animals Can Teach Us about Spirituality: Inspiring Lessons from Wild and Tame Creatures *by Diana L. Guerrero* 6 x 9, 176 pp, Quality PB, 978-1-893361-84-3 **$16.95**

Spirituality

Awakening the Spirit, Inspiring the Soul
30 Stories of Interspiritual Discovery in the Community of Faiths
Edited by Brother Wayne Teasdale and Martha Howard, MD; Foreword by Joan Borysenko, PhD
Thirty original spiritual mini-autobiographies showcase the varied ways that people come to faith—and what that means—in today's multi-religious world.
6 x 9, 224 pp, HC, 978-1-59473-039-9 **$21.99**

The Alphabet of Paradise: An A–Z of Spirituality for Everyday Life
by Howard Cooper 5 x 7¼, 224 pp, Quality PB, 978-1-893361-80-5 **$16.95**

Creating a Spiritual Retirement: A Guide to the Unseen Possibilities in Our Lives
by Molly Srode 6 x 9, 208 pp, b/w photos, Quality PB, 978-1-59473-050-4 **$14.99**
HC, 978-1-893361-75-1 **$19.95**

Finding Hope: Cultivating God's Gift of a Hopeful Spirit
by Marcia Ford 8 x 8, 200 pp, Quality PB, 978-1-59473-211-9 **$16.99**

The Geography of Faith: Underground Conversations on Religious, Political and Social Change *by Daniel Berrigan and Robert Coles* 6 x 9, 224 pp, Quality PB, 978-1-893361-40-9 **$16.95**

God Within: Our Spiritual Future—As Told by Today's New Adults *Edited by Jon M. Sweeney and the Editors at SkyLight Paths* 6 x 9, 176 pp, Quality PB, 978-1-893361-15-7 **$14.95**

Spirituality & Crafts

The Knitting Way: A Guide to Spiritual Self-Discovery
by Linda Skolnik and Janice MacDaniels
7 x 9, 240 pp, Quality PB, b/w photographs, 978-1-59473-079-5 **$16.99**

The Quilting Path: A Guide to Spiritual Discovery through Fabric, Thread and Kabbalah
by Louise Silk
7 x 9, 192 pp, Quality PB, b/w photographs and illustrations, 978-1-59473-206-5 **$16.99**

The Scrapbooking Journey: A Hands-On Guide to Spiritual Discovery
by Cory Richardson-Lauve; Foreword by Stacy Julian
7 x 9, 176 pp, Quality PB, 8-page full-color insert, plus b/w photographs
978-1-59473-216-4 **$18.99**

Spiritual Practice

Divining the Body: Reclaim the Holiness of Your Physical Self
by Jan Phillips
A practical and inspiring guidebook for connecting the body and soul in spiritual practice. Leads you into a milieu of reverence, mystery and delight, helping you discover your body as a pathway to the Divine.
8 x 8, 256 pp, Quality PB, 978-1-59473-080-1 **$16.99**

Finding Time for the Timeless: Spirituality in the Workweek
by John McQuiston II
Simple, refreshing stories that provide you with examples of how you can refocus and enrich your daily life using prayer or meditation, ritual and other forms of spiritual practice. 5½ x 6¾, 208 pp, HC, 978-1-59473-035-1 **$17.99**

The Gospel of Thomas: A Guidebook for Spiritual Practice
by Ron Miller; Translations by Stevan Davies
An innovative guide to bring a new spiritual classic into daily life.
6 x 9, 160 pp, Quality PB, 978-1-59473-047-4 **$14.99**

Earth, Water, Fire, and Air: Essential Ways of Connecting to Spirit
by Cait Johnson 6 x 9, 224 pp, HC, 978-1-89336l-65-2 **$19.95**

Labyrinths from the Outside In: Walking to Spiritual Insight—A Beginner's Guide
by Donna Schaper and Carole Ann Camp
6 x 9, 208 pp, b/w illus. and photos, Quality PB, 978-1-893361-18-8 **$16.95**

Practicing the Sacred Art of Listening: A Guide to Enrich Your Relationships
and Kindle Your Spiritual Life—The Listening Center Workshop
by Kay Lindahl 8 x 8, 176 pp, Quality PB, 978-1-893361-85-0 **$16.95**

Releasing the Creative Spirit: Unleash the Creativity in Your Life
by Dan Wakefield 7 x 10, 256 pp, Quality PB, 978-1-893361-36-2 **$16.95**

The Sacred Art of Bowing: Preparing to Practice
by Andi Young 5½ x 8½, 128 pp, b/w illus., Quality PB, 978-1-893361-82-9 **$14.95**

The Sacred Art of Chant: Preparing to Practice
by Ana Hernández 5½ x 8½, 192 pp, Quality PB, 978-1-59473-036-8 **$15.99**

The Sacred Art of Fasting: Preparing to Practice
by Thomas Ryan, CSP 5½ x 8½, 192 pp, Quality PB, 978-1-59473-078-8 **$15.99**

The Sacred Art of Forgiveness: Forgiving Ourselves and Others through God's Grace
by Marcia Ford 8 x 8, 176 pp, Quality PB, 978-1-59473-175-4 **$16.99**

The Sacred Art of Listening: Forty Reflections for Cultivating a Spiritual Practice
by Kay Lindahl; Illustrations by Amy Schnapper
8 x 8, 160 pp, b/w illus., Quality PB, 978-1-893361-44-7 **$16.99**

The Sacred Art of Lovingkindness: Preparing to Practice
by Rabbi Rami Shapiro; Foreword by Marcia Ford
5½ x 8½, 176 pp, Quality PB, 978-1-59473-151-8 **$16.99**

Sacred Speech: A Practical Guide for Keeping Spirit in Your Speech
by Rev. Donna Schaper 6 x 9, 176 pp, Quality PB, 978-1-59473-068-9 **$15.99**
HC, 978-1-893361-74-4 **$21.95**

About SKYLIGHT PATHS Publishing

SkyLight Paths Publishing is creating a place where people of different spiritual traditions come together for challenge and inspiration, a place where we can help each other understand the mystery that lies at the heart of our existence.

Through spirituality, our religious beliefs are increasingly becoming a part of our lives—rather than *apart* from our lives. While many of us may be more interested than ever in spiritual growth, we may be less firmly planted in traditional religion. Yet, we do want to deepen our relationship to the sacred, to learn from our own as well as from other faith traditions, and to practice in new ways.

SkyLight Paths sees both believers and seekers as a community that increasingly transcends traditional boundaries of religion and denomination—people wanting to learn from each other, *walking together, finding the way.*

For your information and convenience, at the back of this book we have provided a list of other SkyLight Paths books you might find interesting and useful. They cover the following subjects:

Buddhism / Zen	Gnosticism	Mysticism
Catholicism	Hinduism /	Poetry
Children's Books	Vedanta	Prayer
Christianity	Inspiration	Religious Etiquette
Comparative	Islam / Sufism	Retirement
Religion	Judaism / Kabbalah /	Spiritual Biography
Current Events	Enneagram	Spiritual Direction
Earth-Based	Meditation	Spirituality
Spirituality	Midrash Fiction	Women's Interest
Global Spiritual	Monasticism	Worship
Perspectives		

Or phone, fax, mail or e-mail to: SKYLIGHT PATHS Publishing
Sunset Farm Offices, Route 4 • P.O. Box 237 • Woodstock, Vermont 05091
Tel: (802) 457-4000 • Fax: (802) 457-4004 • www.skylightpaths.com
Credit card orders: (800) 962-4544 (8:30AM–5:30PM ET Monday–Friday)
Generous discounts on quantity orders. SATISFACTION GUARANTEED. Prices subject to change.

16.99 7/07